About the Author

Sarah Ivens is the best-selling author of eight lifestyle and wellness books, including *A Modern Girl's Guide to Getting Hitched* and *A Modern Girl's Guide to Etiquette*, and she is the founding Editor in Chief of *OK!* magazine in the US.

A Londoner turned Southern belle, she now splits her time between Austin, Texas and England, after five years in New York, where she ran *OK!*, and two years in Los Angeles, where she worked for the drama development team at HBO television and trained as a certified life coach.

She is currently a PhD candidate in global humanities at the University of Louisville, Kentucky, and is a contributor to the *Daily Mail*, the *Daily Telegraph*, *Stella*, *Glamour*, *Marie Claire*, the *New York Post* and *YOU* magazine. She has worked on staff at *Tatler*, the *Daily Mail*, *Marie Claire* and the *Sunday Mirror*.

The above books by Sarah are published by Piatkus, in addition to *A Modern Girl's Guide to Dynamic Dating*, *A Modern Girl's Guide to the Perfect Single Life*, *A Modern Girl's Guide to Getting Organised*, *A Modern Girl's Guide to Networking* and *The Bride's Guide to Unique Weddings*. *No Regrets: 101 Fabulous Things to Do Before You're Too Old, Married or Pregnant* is published by Random House.

FOREST THERAPY

*Seasonal Ways to Embrace Nature
for a Happier You*

SARAH IVENS

piatkus

PIATKUS

First published in Great Britain in 2018 by Piatkus

1 3 5 7 9 10 8 6 4 2

A CIP catalogue record for this book
is available from the British Library.

ISBN 978-0-349-41889-6

Typeset in Swift by M Rules
Printed and bound in Great Britain by
Clays Ltd, St Ives plc

Papers used by Piatkus are from well-managed forests
and other responsible sources.

Piatkus
An imprint of
Little, Brown Book Group
Carmelite House
50 Victoria Embankment
London EC4Y 0DZ

An Hachette UK Company
www.hachette.co.uk

www.improvementzone.co.uk

For William and Matilda, the most magical gifts
Mother Nature could have bestowed on me, and in loving
memory of my grandma, Mollie Guillaume, who taught
me about gratitude, strength and kindness,
and whom I miss every single day.

Contents

Contents

Introduction

'There is pleasure in the pathless woods, there is
rapture in the lonely shore, there is society where none
intrudes, by the deep sea, and music in its roar;
I love not Man the less, but Nature more.'

Lord Byron

Who hasn't felt happier after a walk in the woods, a picnic in
a park, or a swim in the sea? No one. There is something soul-
soothingly simple and refreshing about being in nature, about
making good use of the great outdoors, in being mindful of
Mother Nature's gifts and grabbing the spring and summer –
and those blue-sky, brisk days of autumn and winter – with
both hands. But, sadly, these are skills we are losing. We are
becoming creatures wrapped in walls and trapped by to-do lists,
hibernating while the world sprouts, grows and changes. Oh,
just think about what we are missing! We are missing out on the
refreshing scent of pine and freshly mown grass. We are missing
getting caught in a shower of pink blossom in spring and being
dazzled by the dusky beauty of roses in late summer. Being in
nature allows us the childlike fun you feel marching through
squelchy mud in autumn or sliding over a glittering world

on a frosty winter's morning. Being in nature is about being attuned to changing seasons and benefitting from the natural world around you. It's the feel of a velvety petal, the sound of a squeaky-smooth grass blade, the sight of dancing dandelion seeds. It's about being present and alive, and never missing out.

But at the moment, we *are* missing out. We're staying in and losing out, and that is making us sad, anxious – and worse. I know, because it happened to me.

As a child, being outdoors was second nature. I was born in Waltham Forest, the London Borough famous, and protected, for the woodlands in which Henry VIII and Elizabeth I used to escape the trials and tantrums of the royal court. I spent most of my time stuck in mud and mushing fallen petals into perfume, or pretending to get married to the neighbour's son under the cherry blossom tree in our back garden. Children are natural, instinctively mindful of their world, and as I went through the turbulence of my parents' divorce, I remember finding solace in the world I had created in the ponds and thickets surrounding my home. I watched tadpoles sprout legs and baby birds gratefully receive their lunch from their busy mothers' beaks, and – despite the adult noise – I was happy.

At 11, my mum and her new husband moved my baby brother and me out to Essex, to a house that backed on to Epping Forest, and a road – quite magically and prophetically – called Sylvan Way. The beauty of trees took on a different importance then. I spent many of my teenage hours among them, but back then the forest was a place to challenge myself away from adult rules and interference: my mates and I gathered there and experimented with making Ouija boards, kissing cute boys and choking on sneaked cigarettes. Now, as an adult, I can see how these green-teen afternoons, roaming the outdoors with my forever friends, shaped me. In the woods, I found my feet and experienced freedom for the first time.

But when I reached my twenties, I moved back to the angry, concrete maze that is London and started spending all my time commuting to grey cubicles through dirty, stuffy underground tunnels. When I was feeling my most toxic and dulled, in an unhappy marriage and dealing with a bullying boss, I visited an aura reader for a magazine article I was researching. She said, 'Your aura is green but struggling with the energy around it. You need to get out into the countryside, take your shoes off, and wriggle grass beneath your toes. It will save your soul.' I ignored her, obviously. I was too busy for pastoral pleasures.

In 2005, at the age of 29, I moved to an even angrier, concrete animal, New York City, to run a weekly magazine – eating all three meals of the day in the office, and relying on fake stimulants like espresso and slices of pizza to survive. I was grey; my life was grey. I hired a yoga teacher (and took classes in my grey apartment) but I was not healthy. Green was not to be seen, apart from in the beer at the St Patrick's Day parade that lurched its way through Manhattan every spring. My marriage fell apart, I got divorced and I collapsed emotionally. A friend gathered me up and shipped me to a retreat in Mexico, where our days were ruled by the rising and falling sun, silent beach walks and bike rides through luxuriant forests to the water-filled sinkholes, known as cenotes. While we picked fresh fruit from trees and put flowers in our hair, I picked myself up. Nature had replenished my broken heart with sea shells, coconut water and the scent of frangipani.

I witnessed the power of nature again in 2010, aged 34, when I took time off work to travel around Asia for three months with my second husband, Russell. We'd been struggling to get pregnant for about 18 months and this was a fertility tour of sorts, to de-stress and think about our options while looking after ourselves and being together. We wanted to re-engage with each other and the world. In Indonesia, I went to Elizabeth Gilbert's Balinese guru from *Eat, Pray, Love* to ask for help. He told me that if I relaxed, meditated, got in touch with nature and opened a nail salon, I would have two children. Spoiler alert: I now have two children but I am not a manicurist.

My most meaningful experience, however, happened in Japan a few months later, in the lush grounds of a Kyoto temple, where a local guide told me to walk leisurely through the bamboo trees in silence, stopping to smell the moss or to feel the suppleness of the different-shaped leaves.

I felt like an Asian-inspired Wordsworth, meditating as I walked the undulating path, my senses hugged by a falling confetti of cherry blossom. I could feel the anxiety, caused by months of worrying whether I would ever be able to conceive a child or not, drift away as I allowed myself to be washed in green. It was a powerful feeling, and one I decided to try to bring home with me. Thirteen months later, I gave birth to my son.

I reconnected with nature in a meaningful, life-saving way, and *Forest Therapy: Seasonal Ways to Embrace Nature for a Happier You* will help you to, too. It offers a simple prescription for a better life: get al fresco! A lot of what I will share with you is common sense; you simply need to be reminded about it. It's a return to a way of living that previous generations – heck, even our parents – embraced more than we are now, and it's paired with the wealth of research into mental, physical and emotional health that is now available to us.

Why nature rocks

These are just some of the benefits that scientists, academics and teachers have discovered occur when a person gets some forest therapy into their life. A life in the great outdoors:

- Reduces blood pressure and heart rate
- Reduces anxiety, anger, depression, obesity, PTSD (post-traumatic stress disorder) and ADHD (attention deficit hyperactivity disorder)
- Restores focus and attention span
- Improves sleep
- Strengthens the immune system
- Increases natural killer cell activity that fights tumours and cancer
- Increases energy and vitality
- Increases sensory awareness and perception
- Promotes a healthy body–mind–heart connection
- Increases brain power and clarity of thought
- Increases self-esteem, empathy, kindness and compassion
- Boosts creativity and intuition
- Increases feelings of awe, wonder and gratitude
- Fosters healthier ageing
- Instils a love of nature and an ecological mindset
- Calms the nervous system
- Relaxes an overworked brain

Today, I'm no fitness bunny; I'm still a bookish nerd with a penchant for cheese sandwiches and Ferrero Rocher, so don't for a minute imagine this book will demand the impossible and be nauseatingly earthy-crunchy or worthy. But the mental and physical health benefits of being outdoors were too persuasive to ignore – even for someone like me – and my family and I have worked hard to fit more nature into our lives. I take weekly walks with friends instead of sitting in a coffee shop. I have romantic *friluftsliv* (a lovely word for the Scandinavian philosophy of outdoor life) moments with my husband. (This week we took a sunset stroll to the top of a beauty spot to watch the International Space Station fly past – see, I'm still a nerd – instead of usual date-night dining.) When it's safe, I take solo strolls along the creek near to my home to process my thoughts, dilemmas and to-do lists. All of these changes to my lifestyle have benefitted my relationships and myself no end.

The intent of these next 12 chapters is to encourage you and your loved ones to get outdoors with the specific intention of connecting with nature in a healing way, to open all the senses, and dynamically interact with the land, whether a city park or a country forest. The pages are filled with an elixir of sound judgement backed by science, inspirational anecdotes brimming with the feel-good factor and easy-to-do, fun ideas to tackle a long list of modern-day dilemmas, from fighting the 'indoor childhood' crisis that's harming our kids, to beating stress, to improving your complexion. And best of all, this essential cure – forest therapy and getting outdoors – is free and suitable for all ages.

Learning to fit more nature into your life should not be a race or a challenge; there isn't a distance marker you have to tick off, no pedometer to check, but the longer one devotes to it, over time, the more beneficial the relationship becomes. *Forest Therapy* is definitely not written for wilderness men, cowgirls, mountain climbers, or white-river rafters. This isn't the book for adrenalin junkies, competitive runners, or speed demons – or for hylophobics (people who have a phobia of forests), for that matter. But it is written for people who find themselves in all types of toxic environments or dead ends and want to live better. Urban dwellers might try to argue that there is nowhere to connect with nature near them, but they should think creatively. Parks, city farms, museums, galleries or the grounds of historic landmarks, retirement home gardens, and so on, you don't need the Yorkshire Moors or the Redwood Forest to roam around in, you can get your foresty fill wherever there are trees and there is time and good intent.

If we can get behind the principle that being in nature is good for both body and soul, then *Forest Therapy* will help you turn it into a process, a practice, not just something we think sounds nice but we can't make time for. Like yoga, meditation, prayer, working out, participating in a book club, and many other worthy endeavours, developing a meaningful relationship with nature takes time and is deepened by returning again and again throughout the cycles of the seasons. We will all benefit from introducing the outdoors into our weekly routines. We just need to relearn how to do it. We need to be reminded of just how good puddle-jumping, mudcake-baking, tree-climbing, squirrel-chasing, blossom-breathing and forest-foraging feel.

Answers and advice will be given to uninspired fathers

wanting to reconnect with their families, bookworms looking to shake off their cobwebs, cooped-up kids needing to let off steam, stressed-out professionals wanting to stop and smell the flowers, and worn-down mums needing a rejuvenating boost. We all know that getting outside is good for us. Our ancestors did it. We should too. This book will help you live your most unforgettable, fabulous al fresco life, because nature really is the best medicine.

1

Sold on Science and Statistics

'Look deep into nature, and then you will understand everything better.'

Albert Einstein

There's a wealth of science and statistics to back up why we need the prescription offered in this book immediately. Yes, the benefits of a walk in the woods and a gulp of fresh air might be so commonsensical that it seems nonsensical to turn it into a wellness revolution but, as a generation of parents and partners, worriers and workers, we are lost.

In the UK, parks and playgrounds are noticeably quieter than they were even 20 years ago, and shopping online has become a national pastime. Public Health England has released a study showing that people in the UK are 20 per cent less active today than they were in the 1960s, and if current trends continue, by 2030 we will be 35 per cent less active. They have released a government-endorsed guide for turning around this shocking situation, including asking adults to take part in 150 minutes of moderate physical activity per week, recommending gardening, walking, hiking, cycling, dancing and swimming.

In the US, visits to state and national parks have declined per capita over the same period. Research shared by the Harvard School of Public Health warns us that American adults spend more time in vehicles than outdoors.

We know this can't be good for us on any level, but we are unsure how to reverse it. How can we busy, harassed, city-dwelling, suburban-surviving folk really embrace nature in a deep and meaningful way when we're all so busy staring at our screens and rushing from building to car to building just to keep up with the world around us? How would it even be possible to re-engage with the changing seasons, the sounds of nature, and the tonic of silence?

But we know we have to find a way, right? Because, as well as never having been so discombobulated, we have never been more aware of the need – as we scroll social media or read newspaper headlines alerting us to the dangers of our sedentary, cloistered, indoorsy, electro-obsessed lives – to revert to the ancient rituals of our parents and grandparents, and of our forefathers, to live more simply. And we need to do it now.

I've noticed how making time – even ten minutes a day, if that is all you have – can make a difference. I know personally how hard it can be to put down my phone, turn off the television, and turn down a glass of wine, but I also know that when I do turn off from these man-made distractions to take a walk around my garden or take the kids to the park, my mood improves, I have more energy and I'm definitely a less stressed-out human being.

Mother Earth loves Mother Nature

All around the world, people are starting to put names and practices to the art of reconnecting with flora and fauna. Facts and figures about the importance of nature to our mental and physical well-being started to emerge on a global stage when it was introduced as part of a public-health programme in Japan in 1982. The Japanese Ministry of Agriculture, Forestry and Fisheries coined the phrase *shinrin-yoku* (translated into English as 'forest bathing') and turned the idea of taking a mindful, elevated nature walk into a national pastime; one that would enhance health, wellness and happiness when participants opened all five senses to their sylvan surroundings, breathed deeply and walked thoughtfully, connecting with nature at a pace that allowed healing. Over the subsequent eight years, Japanese officials spent millions studying the physiological and psychological effects of *shinrin-yoku*, and uncovered positive effects on immunity, blood pressure and stress levels that could last up to a month following each 'bath' in the woods. This led them to designate 48 therapy trails specifically for the purpose.

Elsewhere, wellness experts are on to this very real need, with tree-bathing clubs and mindfulness nature-walk programmes sweeping the most fashionable parts of the United States as well as the stressed bigger cities and the country hippy havens of the United Kingdom. The re-emergence of the

Scandi-trend of *friluftsliv* (translated as 'free-air life') is pushing *hygge*-minded folk out into the world again all over Europe.

In 2017, the United Nations' World Happiness Report declared Norway to be the happiest country on earth, with the government's focus on physical and mental health and freedom considered determining factors, as well as the emphasis on creating positive social spaces that bring people together in nature, like parks and nature reserves. In the same report, the United States came fourteenth, Ireland fifteenth and the United Kingdom nineteenth. Surely this tells us something? That we not only have things to learn from our Norwegian neighbours but that our 21st-century national psyches need to be reconfigured too, to include more outdoor living, social support and focus on self-care, mental health and feeling better and stronger using what is available to us. We may be richer financially that Norway, but we have some catching up to do where it matters: in the wealth of happiness.

Inger, 55

'In Norway, nature is omnipresent and needs to be constantly engaged with. Any Norwegian worth their salt will say, "There is no such thing as bad weather, just bad clothes. Put on an anorak and get outside." Nature is revered and shapes every aspect of Norwegian life, all year round. The word *friluftsliv* embodies this Norwegian philosophy and our connectedness to the outdoors. Freedom. Fresh air. A good life. I feel grateful to have grown up in this culture, and I am passing it down to my children in everything we do.'

Governmental and educational agendas all over the world show just how valuable new facts and figures on reconnecting with nature are and how they are being used to help all sectors of society. This is a global need – and it's growing. Here are a few key examples:

The Natural Resources Institute Finland have set up a government-endorsed, suggested programme of spending five hours in nature per month, to help with the country's struggles with depression and alcoholism, after a government-funded study found psychological improvements in those who spent time outside.

In South Korea, the country's Forest Service offers events such as woodcrafts for cancer patients, prenatal forest meditation

and camping adventures for bullied children, all in their official healing forests, designed to help their citizens feel better
and to lower state medical costs. Prevention is key, and nature
is key to prevention, the Korean government has discovered.
There are dozens of these healing forests around the country
with the inhabitants of most major towns having easy access
to them.

In Switzerland, teachers are setting up *Waldkindergärtens* –
forest playschools – to set their youngsters off on the right track
by encouraging learning through meaningful interactions with
the living world rather than focusing on strict academic criteria.
They are seeing excellent results.

The state of New York, a place synonymous with skyscrapers
and stress, has a guide for residents on its official government
website called 'Immerse Yourself in a Forest for Better Health'.
Those in the Big Apple know their lifestyle is taking a big, bad
bite out of their life and that things need to change.

Into the woods

The benefits of forest therapy in part, it is suggested, are due
to various essential oils that are derived from plants; when
grouped together these are called phytoncides. These are air-
borne chemicals with antibacterial and antifungal qualities
that plants and trees emit to protect themselves from germs
and insects. But phytoncides aren't merely selfish lifesavers looking after only themselves. Forest air doesn't just *feel* fresher and

better for us, scientists now know that it actually *is* better for us. Inhaling forest air, fortified with these phytoncides, appears to improve the function of the immune systems of humans too. These tree-produced chemicals are so powerful that our bodies increase the number and activity of natural killer white blood cells – the cells we need to kill tumours and viruses in the body – when we breathe them in. And that's just the beginning of this forest fairy tale.

A name is just a name

Shakespeare knew that 'a rose by any other name would smell as sweet', and forest therapy by any other name is just as effective!

Italy: al fresco
Japan: *shinrin-yoku*
Norway: *friluftsliv*
South Korea: *sanlimyok*
Spain: *baños de bosque*
UK: forest therapy
US: tree bathing

Top ten woodland winners

Walking in a forest feels good and smells good, and we know we should be doing it. Here's an evergreen list of reasons why trees are terrific. Even if you can't get to a forest, studies show that just taking a walk in a city park or along a tree-lined street produces many of the same benefits.

1 Reduced mental fatigue We all seem to be obsessed with the mental overload of modern living but we don't know how to reduce it. We're saying yes too often, taking on too much, then thinking about everything too deeply. We are sweating the small stuff and it's exhausting. The good news is that research published in the *Journal of Environmental Psychology* shows that being exposed to restorative environments, such as a forest, lake or beach, restores mental energy and that natural beauty inspires feelings of awe which give a sec-  ondary brain boost. Studies even prove how simply looking at pictures of nature increases our positive thinking, so consider switching the lock-screen photo on your phone to a favourite nature photo from a recent holiday. And more good news on the forest front: spending time looking at plants, birds or any of the small details in the magical living world, enables our brain to switch off and change gears, which allows it to step up and focus better with improved patience when we return to work or study.

Short-term memory also improves after a break in the great outdoors. In a study set up by the University of Michigan, participants were given a memory test, then split into two groups and sent for a walk. On returning to re-sit the exam, the group who were sent for a walk around an arboretum did 20 per cent better the second time round, whereas the participants who walked in a city street showed no improvement. Nature for the win!

2 Increased creativity I used to love those spring days when I was at school, when a teacher would take advantage of good weather and take our class out onto the fields next to the playground. I've often felt that taking my writing or research into a green space with fresh air – even to the bustling, sun-dappled patio of a coffee shop or to a quiet park bench – gives my tired mind a new lease of life. Fresh ideas and new perspectives come quicker to me in the open air, it seems, and now I have a few clues as to why. Environmental psychologists at the University of Michigan investigated how the visual elements of nature – looking at a stream, a sunrise, a butterfly, an ancient tree – affected a person's mental fatigue. They discovered that looking at these soft, natural wonders allowed the brain to recuperate, recover and rest after coping with the human-made assaults of modern living, and then enable it to adopt a fresh approach to problems.

The brain in nature is more open to reflect, daydream and wander, which boosts creativity. The psychologists noted that the benefits of spending time in nature even lasted for a while after heading back indoors, so a stroll in a park before an important brainstorming meeting could be something to think about.

Another study, published in the *Public Library of Science* journal, discovered that people immersed in nature for four days boosted their results in a creative problem-solving test by 50 per cent, suggesting a positive cor-relation between the great outdoors and creativity. What is more, they also cited a decrease in exposure to technology over those four days as a possible contributory factor in the test result. But that's another thing I'm advo-cating for in this book – plus, being obsessed with your televi-sion and laptop is harder when you're taking a forest path to a swimming hole!

3 Upgraded happiness I remember the release I felt as an angst-ridden teen when I blew away the cobwebs of my self-obsessed brain and stepped into something greater than my own worries and insecurities: nature. A chat with a friend during a walk in the forest that backed on to my childhood home, or a solo stroll along the briny sand dunes of Norfolk on our annual family holiday, allowed me time to process problems, sending my doldrums up to the sky and out to the North Sea. And this is a practice we should continue throughout our lives, research shows. A study in *Environmental Science and Technology* found a link between decreased anxi-ety and bad moods with walks in the woods, while another reported that taking a walk outdoors should be prescribed by doctors as a supplement to existing treatments for depressive disorders.

The *Journal of Affective Disorders* released analysis that declared how every green, natural environment (not just forests!) improved mood and self-esteem, a crucial element for personal happiness, and that the presence of water – a lake, a river, the ocean – made the positive effects on happiness even more noticeable.

Researchers at the University of Essex studied people exercising outside and found that just five minutes of physicality in a green space lifted spirits and self-confidence. Researchers from the University of Exeter Medical School studied the health data of 10,000 people who lived in cities and found, after adjusting for income, education and employment, that those living near a green space reported less mental distress.

4 Boosted immunity Can green living really make you feel better? According to science and statistics, yes. Dutch researchers found noticeably lower numbers of cases of 15 diseases and health complaints, including heart disease, asthma and diabetes, in people who lived within half a mile of green space. An international conglomerate of scientists asked 31,000 Toronto residents to fill out a questionnaire about their health and found that those living on tree-lined city blocks had a boost in heart and metabolic health compared with those who lived on a more bare and brutal block. Being in a whirl of phytoncides, with the cellular activity they promote, can also provide a general boost to the immune system, helping to fight off flu, coughs and colds, claims a paper in the *Journal of Environmental Health and Preventative Medicine*, although more research is needed into the relationship between the trees and us.

A study has also revealed how patients heal faster after surgery if they're given a green, natural view from their hospital bed. University of Pittsburgh researchers reported that spinal surgery patients exposed to natural light felt less stress and pain, and took fewer pain medications than those patients who weren't, feeding into an earlier study that showed faster recovery times for those in a hospital room with a view of trees rather than a brick wall. Having spent three days recovering from the birth of a child in each hospital environment, I can verify this. Trees lift the spirits, bricks not so much, especially when you're in discomfort.

5 Expanded exercise and heart health When I had my first child, my mother gave me one piece of advice: 'Get outside every day! Even if you're just taking a walk around your neighbourhood, get out in fresh air and move your body.' It was the best piece of advice she ever gave me, and something I share with other new mums. You may feel like hiding in pyjamas, but getting your limbs moving in the fresh air, seeing other adults, feeling your heart beat a little faster and feeling sunshine on your face is invaluable. Studies show that although you don't need to be outside to be active (walking on a treadmill for three miles will burn the same number of calories as walking a forest trail for three miles), your body and brain report extra boosts from moving your workout from a human-made gym to a natural one. British researchers studied 1,000 British children using accelerators and positioning devices and found that children were twice as active outdoors than indoors, highlighting how nature puts an extra spring in our step. The best thing about exercising outdoors is, of course, that it often doesn't feel like exercise, which makes it more sustainable as a way of life rather than just a passing fad in a bid to lose weight. A power walk around a local park with a friend, checking out the changing seasons as you march under canopies of trees, fresh air plumping up your tired skin, is more invigorating, social and interesting than solo gym time, watching the clock obsessively as icy air conditioning blasts in your face.

6 Diminished stress And breathe … nature is a wondrous soother. Many studies show that exercising in forests – or even just sitting in one – reduces blood pressure and decreases the stress-related hormones cortisol and adrenalin, which helps us to calm down. Even looking at photos or drawings of trees has a similar effect – and that's why the screensaver on my work computer is an image of California's Muir Woods.

One study published in the *Biomedical and Environmental Sciences* journal showed that a view of nature outside the window lowered stress and increased job satisfaction among workers. Another study from the *Scandinavian Journal of Forest Research* found that students who were sent into a forest to camp for two days returned with significantly lower levels of cortisol in their system than those who had stayed in the city, and researchers at *Environmental Health and Preventative Medicine* had similar results, noting that both cortisol levels and heart rate decreased for people spending time away from a city environment and in a place of forest therapy.

7 Sharper vision Carrots aren't the only natural thing to help your vision, studies show. Common sense tells us it's good to get away from the glare of a computer screen, but there could be more to it than that. An Australian study looked at 2,000 children over a period of two years and found that those who spent more time outdoors had a reduced risk of developing near-sightedness (myopia). In Taiwan, researchers looked at two neighbouring schools with comparable levels of myopia. Over the period of a year, one school was encouraged to play outside more. The results? Testing the children after 12 months, the data revealed the outdoor kids had a rate of myopia of 8.41 per cent, compared to 17.65 per cent in the indoor kids. Both of these studies were published in the *Ophthalmology* journal and, although focusing on children, they do show a link between the protective effect of outdoor activity on eyesight, and how important it is to exercise your eyesight by looking at things that are far away. Without a horizon, when focused on television screens and trapped within closed walls, children's eyes become lazy. And as adults we get that. Whose eyes haven't felt rested when they're taken off a blinking computer screen for a few minutes?

8 Increased ability to cope with pain I suffer from hormonal migraines, and about 72 hours of each month are wiped out in excruciating pain. During this time, I want to lie silent and still, gripping my way through it alone; however, with two young, rambunctious children, this isn't an option. Instead, I'm forced out on to school runs and park visits. And however hard it is to pull my bones outdoors, my spirits are always lifted. A lungful of fresh air and soothing scenery has a noticeable effect on my headaches. A report by the King's Fund, commissioned by the National Garden's Scheme, has revealed that being outdoors, and gardening specifically, offers the ill and unwell a myriad of physical and psychological benefits as well as natural pain relief.

Horticultural therapy is really a thing, with evidence from clinical trials showing how it can help those with arthritis: the rhythmic turning and twisting of weeding, for example, alleviating discomfort and stiffness. Thrive, a British charity that encourages gardening to help people living with illness or disabilities, offers programmes of horticultural therapy to people dealing with a variety of health issues, including activities for people with dementia designed to help with positive reminiscence, reconnecting with others and gentle exercise. Having recently lost my grandmother to dementia, I saw first-hand how her life in a memory care home was improved by the effort the wonderful staff there made to bring nature into the building – flowers, plants, even baby goats and rabbits – and to encourage the residents to sit outside in the well-tended garden every day.

9 A longer life? It would make sense, knowing what we now know from the studies outlined above, that getting outdoors and embracing all that is green and glorious in nature would reduce the risk of an early death. How could a happier, less stressed, more active life not mean that? Well, luckily, scientists have been working to prove the correlation and have come up with the goods: not only will going outdoors more give you a better life in the here and now but it will also make it a longer one. Dutch researchers, publishing their findings in the *Journal of Epidemiology and Community Health*, wrote that fatal diseases were less prevalent in those who lived in close proximity to green space. Their findings were backed up by a study in *Environmental Health Perspectives*, which uncovered a reduced risk of cancer, kidney disease and lung disease in the people they followed. Both studies show that not only does a positive relationship with the natural world encourage exercise, relaxation and social interaction but it also has a significant effect on mental health, which, the researchers believe, leads to an uptick in overall good health and longevity.

10 And embracing nature makes you a nicer person! I know this first hand. Taking an argument, a grumble or an attitude problem – mine, my husband's or one of my children's – out into the sunlight always brightens and then reduces it. There's no quicker way to ditch those itchy-scratchy irks that have made you mad, angry and not very pleasant to be around than taking a breather, appreciating how beautiful the world is, and becoming aware of how very small this moment in time and our place in it is. And anyway, seriously, how can you be miserable and mean when faced with a glorious sunset or a mother bird making a nest for her chirping offspring? You're not Cruella de Vil – a woman who, by the way, probably never spent any time in a forest!

In a paper called 'Vitalizing effects of being outdoors and

in nature', published in the *Journal of Environmental Psychology*, a group of international psychologists explain how we feel a boost in kindness when we spend time in nature as a result of the happy expression our brains and bodies feel when being in touch with who we really are and what we want to do. Nature, their work explains, makes us feel energised and generous towards others, encouraging us to look outwards instead of inwards. Digging your toes into soil, stroking the flaking bark of an oak tree, looking for a blaze of sunlight through a verdant canopy of leaves – even hanging out your washing on a blustery blue-sky day – reminds us that we are alive and full of possibility. How can we be mean to others when Mother Nature is so generous to us?

Lucy, 29

'It feels ridiculous writing this now, but towards the end of last year I felt I was heading for a breakdown. I was overwhelmed. The stress and pressure of work and home were tying me in knots and I couldn't tell how I was going to be set free. Luckily, I met a new colleague during the peak of my anxiety who suggested that instead of hanging around our desks and gossiping or moaning during our one-hour lunch break, which was the office culture, we went for a walk and talked about anything other than work. Changing that mindset, getting regular exercise and fresh air, and other tweaks I made to my lifestyle, really saved my life from getting very gloomy.'

Come on, get happy – not SAD!

There's no denying that modern life has turned us into an indoor species – and it's making us miserable, especially during the colder months. Seasonal affective disorder (SAD) afflicts an estimated 20 per cent of Brits every winter – when sunshine and natural light are hard to come by – and the symptoms can run from a general feeling of lethargy to debilitating depression. Those suffering from it are told to embrace anything from prescribed light therapy (you sit a few feet away from a light box that mimics natural outdoor light) to antidepressants, to talk therapy. But could there be more to SAD than a simple lack of sunlight?

Richard Louv, an American author and co-founder of the Children and Nature Network, coined the term nature-deficit disorder (NDD) after analysing the negative health effects when there is detachment from the great outdoors. Louv believes it's a disconnection with nature itself – which is more exaggerated during the autumn and winter – that makes us feel sluggish and depressed, and not just the exposure to less sunlight. You won't get a medical diagnosis for NDD, and doctors can't prescribe a woodland hike and a swim in a waterfall – yet – but Louv has identified many shared symptoms between NDD sufferers – a lack of concentration, exhaustion and low moods – and those of the now widely acknowledged problem of SAD, giving us even more reasons to get outside all year round.

Hello sunshine!

We've all felt the warm glow of the sun on our skin, felt embraced by it like a warm hug, and felt happier and healthier because of it, but we've also been scared by the idea of getting too much sun, which promotes skin damage and, in some cases, skin cancer. These fears have almost justified our swing towards the exclusively indoor lifestyle we have today. If we work outside the home, we commute and rush to the office for eight-hour days, perhaps rewarding ourselves with a soulless, uninspiring run on a treadmill afterwards, before heading back to four walls and bed. If we're at home, parenting or working, the chances are we spend more time in front of our washing machines than in our back gardens, on a hamster wheel of domesticity and to-do lists; however, when exposed in a careful, considered way to the rays, the benefits are indisputable.

What's the real deal with sunlight? We've become so cautious about UVA and UVB damage that the British Dietetic Association (BDA) are worried that our dwindling vitamin D levels are making us ill. They've taken the step of announcing a sunshine plan to follow, making getting outdoors three times a week for 15 minutes to top up our 'sunshine vitamin' as much a priority as eating our five fruits and vegetables a day. So, remember, limited sun exposure on short walks paired with the liberal use of sunscreen when you are outside for extended periods of time and/or during the hottest part of the day can increase your wellness. Here are three powerful reasons why:

1 Sunshine increases our levels of serotonin The 'happiness hormone' helps with many common complaints such as depression, headaches and loss of appetite. Antidepressants are often the medical answer to increasing serotonin, but they often have undesirable side effects, such as giving us low libido and low energy. Luckily, Mother Nature lends a hand in the form of vitamin D, which helps to encourage serotonin production and release. Vitamin D is known as the 'sunshine vitamin' because of the process that sunlight hitting the skin promotes in the body. The liver and kidneys absorb the sun's rays and convert them into a biologically active form of this wonder vitamin.

2 Sunshine builds immunity to illnesses A Harvard University Medical School study outlines that while many vitamins are necessary, they don't have the same great disease-fighting powers of vitamin D. Research suggests an appropriate level of vitamin D, from exposure to sunshine or by taking a supplement, may have protective effects against osteoporosis, cancer, depression, heart attacks and strokes.

3 Sunshine helps us to sleep better Exposure to the sun helps to streamline our body's circadian rhythms, allowing us a good night's rest. How much sleep we get – and how refreshing that sleep is – is affected by light, especially sunlight. If your body clock needs to be reset so that you can get some shut-eye at a decent time, getting outdoors in the early part of the day will improve your alertness and energy during the day, and it is likely to help you fall asleep at night.

Your prescription is ready!

In this chapter I've outlined the recognised health and wellness crisis going on today that our modern way of living is promoting: skyrocketing stress and anxiety, vitamin D deficiency, children with ADD (attention deficit disorder) and ADHD (attention deficit hyperactivity disorder), increasing obesity, jumping rates of depression, addiction to smartphones and not-so-smart prescription medication, seasonal affective disorder (SAD) and nature-deficit disorder (NDD).

Facts and figures are revealing, however, that a simple thing like taking regular forest walks and forming a meaningful relationship with the natural world can help to get us all back on the right track.

I still remember the moment when it all came together for me. It was in Mexico in 2008 when I arrived for that life-changing week's retreat as a husk of a professional person with a slow-beating heart, addicted to my email account and exhausted from my insomniac tendencies. I was frazzled and nervous about my future. Time away from the distractions and stresses of the high rises of Manhattan, and staying in a place where BlackBerries and other mobile devices were banned, forced me to think and to analyse what was important.

The camp where I was staying didn't have electricity, so I rose with the sun and went to bed with it too. I took silent beach walks and cycled to swimming holes. On the last bike ride of the trip I felt lighter and brighter, and I remember belting out the Elton John song, 'Someone Saved My Life Tonight', the whole way home, even when the heavens opened and I got soaked, or maybe especially when the heavens opened and I got soaked – something I would never have done before this resetting of my life. (I have a terrible voice; the other holidaymakers probably hated it!) That moment is still one of the happiest of my life; a moment so simple, not as momentous as my wedding day or the birth of my two children, but charming because the joy came from having sun on my skin, blood pumping around my body and my eyes dazzled by the turquoise water of the coastline and the emerald green of the palm leaves overhead. Nature had taught me lessons about my nature that I needed to adopt and nurture.

How tempting this new nature-filled way of living is then, to bathe our senses in the beauty of our universe, to listen, feel, smell and touch it, rather than locking ourselves away in a human-made world. How powerful knowing that our mental and physical health, stress levels, moods and relationships will all improve in nature – and we'll look younger (fresh air and rosy cheeks are guaranteed rejuvenators) into the bargain. In the next chapter I'll discuss ways for you to get outdoors more without it feeling like a struggle.

MINDFULNESS MINUTE

A simple one to start. Take a minute in your garden, in a park, or in a forest and repeat to yourself: 'I inhale the future, I exhale the past', breathing in and out slowly and deeply, in time with the sentiment, eyes open softly.

2

A Walk in the Woods

'Climb the mountains and get their good tidings. Nature's
peace will flow into you as sunshine flows into trees. The winds
will blow their own freshness into you, and the storms their
energy, while cares will drop off like autumn leaves. As
age comes on, one source of enjoyment after another
is closed, but Nature's sources never fail.'

John Muir

First things first – don't freak out. This is a simple practice that
works for all ages, fitness levels and lifestyles. Like yoga, getting some forest therapy and outdoor moving into your life is a
non-competitive practice to be taken at your own pace, with an
agenda you can physically and mentally handle but also enjoy.
Be kind to yourself. Think about all the benefits you'll get. Very
soon getting outdoors and engaging with nature will become,
excuse the pun, second nature.

Seize the day

There are little tweaks you can start doing immediately, even if you haven't got an hour spare to go for a nature walk. Small things such as waking up and not just checking your weather app to see what you should wear that day, but actually looking out the window (radical, huh?), checking the movement of the clouds, how the wind is pushing through the trees, and listening out for local birds beckoning in the morning with a gleeful chorus. At night, don't go straight for the glare of a television screen or YouTube page. Take a moment to look outside, notice the sky changing colour, the visibility of the stars, the sounds of night. It never hurt anyone to disengage from their day with a quiet minute, breathing in the cool night air, calmly preparing for bedtime away from the barrage of entertainment that crowds our lives.

Forest therapy for beginners

You just have to put one foot in front of the other, isn't that how everything starts? But even that can feel nerve-wracking. It's like when I stare at a blank page, all these ideas, stories and characters flourish inside my head, but I have no idea how to write them down, or get them out. So, I nervously tap away – edit and delete – until the right way starts to present itself. I felt the same trying to reconnect with nature after ten-plus years of living, loving and working in concrete, wound-up, grey cities. Engaged again, I knew that the smooth surface of a blade of grass felt good between my fingers and the wash of jasmine on a breezy day sweetened my soul, but I didn't know how to harness them. How would I make nature fit into my life when I already had a long list of other priorities? Over time I realised I couldn't, and shouldn't, try to make nature fit into a schedule like a chore. I had simply to notice her, embrace her and welcome her in every aspect of my life: my exercise routine, my parenting, my relationships.

We can't master Mother Nature and get the most from her. We simply have to go with her flow and at her pace, relinquish control, respect her unpredictability. With her as my guide and common sense as my safety net, the wonders of the great outdoors were easier to grasp. My plans could get rained on. I'd deal with it.

Remember what forest therapy is versus what is isn't

- It is more about melatonin and less about adrenalin.
- It is more about calm and less about competition.
- It is more about natural wonder and less about human-made entertainment.
- It is more about noticing the weather and less about moaning about it.
- It is more about mental gain and less about weight loss.
- It is more about slow healing and less about quick fixes.

Motivators to get moving

1 Set an easy goal to start Don't tell yourself that you have to get out every day or there's no point and that if you miss one session you might as well give up. This isn't marathon training. Once a week is a great way to begin. Once a month is better than nothing.

2 Leave yourself notes and photos around your house to remind you of the beauty and stillness that could be yours. Instead of the ancient photo of you in a bikini you might stick to the fridge to stop you comfort eating during any given diet, pin up the most glorious vista, a magical view of treetops, or put a picture of a verdant mountain landscape next to your toothbrush.

3 Tell people what you've discovered about forest therapy, feed off their energy and commit to this lifestyle change publicly. You might even attract a few suitable fellow foresters in the process.

4 Keep a diary Note how you feel now on all levels: mentally, physically and spiritually. Read through Chapter 1 again and know that things can only improve with this lifestyle change. Keep the diary up to date and register how you feel differently as your forest therapy goes on. (See also Mindfulness minute on page 51.)

5 Sign up to join a nature walking group if you think that will help. Before you even set a step outside, they will be sharing exciting information and encouraging anecdotes about the positive impact forest therapy has had on the other members.

6 Be compassionate – to yourself. Imagine you are talking to your best friend or sibling. What would you say to them if they were in a funk and talked about the idea of starting forest therapy? You'd encourage them, wouldn't you? You'd look forward to hearing how they'd got on. Think about being your own BFF.

7 Visualise the new you happier, more creative, less anxious, and with stronger thighs. You can see it, can't you?

8 Promise yourself a reward Give yourself a loose time frame and make a promise that if you really do spend more time outdoors and less time indoors, valuing the important things and turning off the television more, you'll make a treat of it – book yourself a weekend camping (or preferably glamping), or a picnic with friends, or buy some new plants for your garden.

If you go down in the woods today . . .

- Before heading out for a fruitful forest therapy moment, consider the weather – not to stop you, just to prepare you for all eventualities. Soggy shoes, sunburn or goose-bumped skin will take away from your ability to enjoy the aromas and sensations you discover. Plan ahead by packing relevant weather gear in your backpack. It's always a good idea to pack water and a snack too.

- Although hard-core tree bathers advise against taking a phone, for safety reasons I suggest you might want to – just be stern with yourself and leave it in a pocket. No checking emails or Facebook – and even taking photos should be kept to an absolute minimum; your camera should only be unleashed for truly unique sights. Selfies can be shelved.

- If there's anything that can't wait on your to-do list, get it done before you head into nature or it will suck up all your mental energy. You'll find it easier to switch off and reclaim these minutes for yourself even when you have things on your mind in time, but when you first start getting into the practice of tree bathing, you'll need to clear your mental inbox first.

- Once you arrive – at the park, the forest, the woodland trail – remind yourself that you are not here to hike or race. You are here to breathe and restore a sense of peace within yourself, your relationship or your family. Set an alarm if you need to be somewhere at a certain time. If not, let Father Time take a backseat to Mother Nature.

- If you are sharing this experience with someone else, agree before you set off to make this a silent walk, and that you can share stories and observations during intermittent breaks or at the end. Shush is necessary. Choose your fellow forest bather carefully.

- Silent walks won't be possible if you're walking with children, but you can still set a 'sixty second silence' challenge, adding time as they get used to it. Kids love a game, especially if there's a reward at the end.

- If you are taking this walk alone, observe all usual safety precautions.

- First walk. Tread ahead at your own pace, stop and stroll whenever you want to. Listen to your body and let your feet guide you – what are you gravitating towards? How does your body feel? Breathe steadily. Fill up on those phytoncides.

- Then sit. Find a good spot and go into a restful state. Let thoughts pop into your head and pop out without allowing anything to linger or niggle. Check out the big things – ancient trees, the sky above – then focus on the small: a leaf, a stone. Breathe deeply. Feel the phytoncides flow through your body.

- Observe the usual rules: Don't litter. Don't destroy. Don't take anything that doesn't belong to you. Don't leave anything that could be dangerous to woodland life.

- Away from the woods, look back on the experience and wriggle around in your skin and soul to feel for lasting effects. Were there any? What was your favourite part? Was it worth it? Would you like to do it again? Congratulations. You're officially a forest bather.

Merijayd, 42

'Recently, I was in a period in my life where I was working intensely to get a new business off the ground,
bringing in just enough income to stay afloat while
my husband, who was laid off, looked for a job. I was
giving and spending much energy on everything and
everybody else – I was depleted. So, I decided to go to my
mother. Mother Earth, that is. I put up a hammock in
my back garden and made myself stay put and do nothing for a little while every day. I let the gentle swinging
and the breezes soothe my mind. The gentle compres-
sion of the hammock was like a comforting hug. The
colours of the blue sky, fluffy clouds and rich green
leaves of the pecan trees took me to another place. It
was a place where I was a child running freely in the
grass, making forts in the woods and feeling the support of nature. I knew that my mother would always
give me the peace and the time and space to heal as long
as I let her.'

Sensational senses

A huge part of reconnecting with nature is the chance it gives
you to open up the five senses. As you head into Sylvania, focus
on everything around you and how it makes you feel inside.
Meander or recline and think about the following:

Sound What can you hear as you walk? Listen out for leaves crunching, twigs snapping, water burbling, rocks clashing, wind rustling and creatures scuttling. Can you hear birdsong? Can you hear distinct types of birdsong? Can you tell an owl from a woodpecker? Are there any other animals or insects buzzing or bustling around your path?

On a recent camping trip we were awoken by the noise of the scampering feet of local deer, heading our way to have a nose at us, their new neighbours. It definitely beat being woken up by jackhammering, swearing and sirens – even on Sundays – which had been my alarm for the five years I lived in New York City.

Sight How many different colours can you see? How many strange shapes? Does anything you see remind you of your childhood or your home? Have you seen anything on this walk that you haven't seen before? Can you see any wildlife? Have they left any tracks? Can you see their homes? Are they in family groups or on their own?

On a recent walk, I witnessed a family of turtles sunbathing on a log that had washed up onto the verdant banks of the Colorado River. All the relatives were there – the old grandparents, shells mottled with algae and dents, the smooth teenagers, jumping into the water athletically to cool down and easily hopping up again, and the babies, tiny and nervous, some being piggybacked around by larger ones. I stopped for a good while to watch them, giggling at the family dynamics. If I'd been looking at my phone, I would have missed them.

Touch Climb a tree or rock. How do your hands feel? Is some bark smoother than others? Or some rocks sharper than others? Roll over a log, feel the difference between the dry bark and the moisture underneath it. Forage for different natural objects – hunt out acorns, pine cones, conkers and pine needles. How do they feel? Are they spiky or soft? Roll your found items around in your palm as you close your eyes.

We live in Texas now and I still get a thrill stroking the giant cactus palms, wary of the prickles, or standing next to a palm tree and feeling the fronds waft across my back in the breeze. Of course, though, I do miss the feeling of dangling my fingertips into a cool ocean of bluebells on a stroll through a forest at home in England. Bluebells are hard to come by in the Lone Star State.

Smell Take a deep lungful of the forest. How does it smell? What does it remind you of? How is it different from the smells of your home and garden, the seaside or the city? Pick up some leaves or pine needles and crush them in your palm – what aroma has been released? Do you like it? What does it remind you of? Can you see any flowers? If so, pick some petals and mush them with your fingertips. What scent do you get? What does it remind you of? When my son, William, was one year old and we were living in Los Angeles, our little family took a road trip up the Pacific Coast Highway to Big Sur. I still remember getting out of the car, the heavy black smog of LA hours behind us, and being knocked out by the divine aroma of the surrounding pines. The sleepless nights of new motherhood were knocked out of me, I felt rejuvenated with every sniff. High up on a hill, looking down to the ocean, I felt like myself again for the first time in months.

Taste Caution is the word here. Unless something is obviously edible – you stumble across brambles full of blackberries or raspberries, or you fancy a bit of legal scrumping for apples – educate yourself first. There is a variety of guide books on edible plants to study diligently or you can join a foraging group of experts, or tag along on a mushroom hunting expedition with a specialist. Another fun thing to do is to pick some forest treats and take them home for tea – fresh, woody teas, like pine-needle tea and stinging-nettle tea, are certainly an acquired taste but fun to experiment with.

Hobby lobby

If you are tempted to use your valuable spare time in nature enhancing your other favourite pastimes, I vote to go for it, as an add-on to your mindful walk and rest. If you're into nature photography, snap away. If you like to paint, take a pad of watercolour paper and watercolours. Write – what could be more inspiring? If you want to step up your workouts outside in a green gym, do that too. The ▶

purpose of forest therapy isn't to get fit, but while you're there, if you want to, burn some calories and build that muscle. There are few things in life not enhanced by being outdoors. Knitting, crocheting, reading, Sudoku ... any of the above will benefit from the natural boost you're giving your body and brain when you are outside.

Take a breather

Inspired by the calm and stillness of the forest, you might want to try a moment of meditation to still yourself. Here are a few pointers for beginners, or indoor meditators nervous about taking the practice outside.

- Find a comfortable spot. That twig digging in one bottom cheek. That rock digging in the other. Nope. They're not going to suddenly feel better. They are a distraction. Take a minute to find the right spot: a spot where you can relax into all good things.
- Hide anything valuable. Yes, you're engaging in the majesty of the natural world, but you have to be sensible. Keep your purse, keys, and so on, in your pocket or in your shoe. Sit on your rucksack.
- Relax your body. Close your eyes. Move around your being from toe to top. Push a chilled-out vibe into each area. Feel for niggles and mentally smooth them out. Shake out your shoulders. Straighten your spine. Let

your jaw slacken. Lastly, focus on your face: make sure you're not holding on to any tension in your eye sockets or around your mouth.

- The crucial part of all this, of course, is to breathe properly – and by that, I mean rhythmically, quietly and deeply. Fill your lungs without forcing anything. Think about how the phytoncide-filled oxygen is flowing around each part of you, lubricating the stiffness and worries away.

- If you want a mantra, a phrase that you repeat to inspire well-being, choose one. It can be anything from the simple 'breathe in and breathe out' to keep you focused on breathing, to some out-there earthy-crunchy line such as, 'I am this forest, I am rooted to this earth, my ancestors are the sky above my head, my feet are on the ground and I am grateful.' Go for it. No one ever has to know what you say to inspire yourself. Go full-on Oprah if it helps.

- Don't allow yourself to be judged. Ignore onlookers. Do your thing because you're doing a good thing. This is worth remembering in general, not just while getting your hippy on in a forest.

And repeat – often if you can.

Taking the trees home

After a wonderfully deep immersion in a forest bath, you might want to try for a secondary sylvan-scented bath in your tub at home. A host of woody essential oils will bring the forest through your front door and into your bathroom. Root your relaxation by pouring yourself a warm, fragrant bath for a relaxing soak, burning oils in an infuser, or lighting a candle next to it while you unwind, flame flickering away, or by massaging the oil into your slightly damp skin (check how potent the oil is first; you may need to blend it with a body cream).

Aromatherapy has never smelt so good – and bonus, many of the phytoncides that mingle in the forest find their way into the essential oil bottle, so it doesn't just feel like the oils are doing you good, they really are. Essentially (geddit?), working with these woodland oils will give you similar advan-

tages to taking some time out in nature, including reduced stress, raised concentration, improved mood and reduced insomnia. Get pouring and sniffing, and remember – the purer the oil the more powerful it is.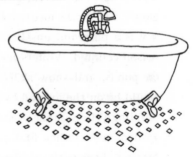

Birch The antibacterial powerhouse
Cedar wood The muscle relaxer
Cypress The lung opener
Fir needle The blood-pressure leveller
Juniper The confidence booster
Pine The immunity booster
Sandalwood The spirit lifter
Spruce The pain reliever
White fir The stress reducer

For a floral fix, if you need a quick lift, add a couple of drops of your favourite oil to a tissue and sniff. If you feel that a boost at work could be advantageous to you and your colleagues, add a few drops to a fine-mist spray bottle and fill with filtered water. Spray around you, your desk, your grumpy boss or competitive colleague for an undisputable reboot.

Deborah, 50

'I grew up in the seventies. The outside was our video game, our social media, our mall, our everything. It was a pure and unselfconscious playground. Each season counted. Winters meant sledging and skating on ponds, and snow skies that foreshadowed what would be on the ground by morning. Spring was the blinding yellow bands of the forsythia hedges in our garden, my mother finding abandoned robins and feeding them with eye droppers of milk until they could be launched back into the wild. Summers meant tramping through local woods, pulling honeysuckle apart to suck out a tiny drop of nectar, feeling lucky if a ladybird landed on us. The trauma of bee stings, the annoyance of mosquitoes. Trying and sometimes succeeding at lighting fires with magnifying glasses. Raking leaves was the thing in autumn. The smells of every season: the smells that identified so much and that we were taught so casually in the language of our parents and grandparents.'

Money does grow on trees

The great outdoors is the great equaliser – free air and free
fun await. We're too hung up these days on thinking we
need to book events, buy tickets and be seen. Rubbish. A
number of times I've paid for some big thing for my children
to experience only to find them having more fun with a
friend in a puddle as they're leaving the venue. Get out of
the mindset that paying means better and planning is necessary. Think back. I bet some of your best days have been
spontaneous, haphazard, wild and free – in both senses of
the word. Think outside the box (and by box, I mean building) when planning your next excursion and see how much
healthier your bank balance becomes.

MINDFULNESS MINUTE

Keep a sunrise or sunset diary by your bed. Choose which one according to your schedule and sleep cycle. Each morning or evening take 60 seconds to appreciate the beginning or end of the day by saying hello or goodbye to the sun, noting in your book how the sky looked and how you felt: good or bad, calm or anxious. Acknowledging your feelings and reflecting on them can help us to gain power over them, and linking them to something as powerful as the sun and the cycle of the day acts as a good reminder that we all get fresh starts every 24 hours and that this world is bigger than us.

3

Spring Cleaning

'Spring drew on ... and a greenness grew over those
brown beds, which, freshening daily, suggested the thought
that Hope traversed them at night, and left each
morning brighter traces of her steps.'

Charlotte Brontë

Ah, spring. The smell of green grass pervades your nostrils,
dazzling sunlight sneaks through your blinds in the morning –
at last! – for a natural wake-up call, while the dampness of dew
cleans away the problems of the day before. Even as a child, in
a narrow world focused on Jem dolls and glittery leg warmers,
I remember the excitement spring brought with it. The air felt
lighter and brighter, and we all – flora, fauna and human – got
a boost from the longer days and warmer weather after the
bleakness of winter. There were moments in my childhood
when a bunch of daffodils felt like so much more than a
handful of flowers. They were a peace offering, a mum-tamer,

a cup of sunshine brightening a disrupted home, a gathering of gold crowns promising me a glowing future. Even now, as a more cynical and haggard fortysomething, spring brings optimism. Being out in nature to watch and connect with the sprouting, growing, blooming and blossoming of this season only exaggerates the positivity available to us.

Why is spring so special?

When a season is as green and grassy, fresh and fragrant, and fertile and fabulous as spring is, it's only right that it should be celebrated and adored. After the spring equinox, the days get longer and the nights get shorter, which makes us feel that more is possible. The deep freeze of winter is over, but the dryness of summer is still in the distant future. Migrating birds return to trees in triumphant chirps – they have survived, and so have you. Baby animals are born and chicks hatch, new eyes blinking out into the world. There are new heads to be turned to see the trees as they once again sprout their leaves – their fruit – and the world turns green.

On top of all this lush 'n' leafy stuff, as if Mother Nature hasn't already handed us enough to be happy about, there is a plethora of bank holiday weekends to enjoy. There are pancakes on Shrove Tuesday and good luck on St Patrick's Day, plus cute bunnies and fluffy ducklings – both chocolate and real – to coo over at Easter.

It is also famously the time of year when we see out the old and bring in the new, physically, mentally and emotionally. Spring is the time of increased light and increased heat, two things that rev up our minds and bodies. The earth has come to life again, and you feel you can too. To harness the natural power of spring is to feel strong and full of potential, to feel the ability to grow and bloom from your head to your toes. How can you use this season's wonderful ways to improve your life, happiness and relationship with the living world?

Emerge from your cocoon

Detoxing after colder weather, shorter days and the traditionally overindulgent nights of the festive season can take some work. Eggnog can leave you groggy, and perhaps that last mince pie was a step too far. It feels easier to slump onto the couch for a box-set marathon than to step out, wide-eyed and blinking, into a brave, new world. You might feel sluggish and dull, but help is at hand from Mother Nature. Fling open your windows – house, car, office – and let the fresh air circulate. Pack away the *hygge*-home-helpers (cashmere socks, woolly blankets and fir-scented candles) that have hijacked your home since December and replace them with bowls of fresh fruit, vases of fragrant flowers and window boxes filled to brimming with bulbs. Each new day is a new beginning in spring, and forging strong connections with nature – something as simple as watching the bulbs burst and bloom from your kitchen

window – will connect you to it and bring you great, simple, unadulterated pleasure.

Spring awakening

Researchers from Sussex University tested the brain activity of 17 healthy subjects listening to a variety of natural and unnatural soundscapes. When asked about how the sounds affected them, the participants reported that the natural sounds led to relaxation and a feeling of positivity, whereas the unnatural sounds made them feel stressed. Brain scans taken just afterwards backed this up, with researchers noting how artificial sounds activated anxiety-related brain activity. So, introduce a spring chorus of birdsong through an open window into your morning routine and turn off the television news. It'll give you a much calmer start to your day.

Shake off your hibernation hangover

The first thing you can do to shake off the previous season and get in step with the new one is to give your wardrobe a thorough edit. The weather will still be changeable and tempestuous, so don't pack your warm things away, just move the heavy, dark stuff to a corner and let the rest of your cupboard flourish in a fiesta of spring shades. Treat yourself to a few new things if you can, just accents like scarves, necklaces or tights will do.

Add apple green, cowslip yellow, crocus mauve and duck-egg blue. These light colours calm the soul and suit most skin tones, and they add a fresh edge to a winter uniform of blacks, dark blues and greys. Think about changing your perfume now too – experiment with floral scents where only the tiniest splash will sweeten your day.

Fling, fix or find it a home

The most rewarding part of spring cleaning your life is to take a proper look at all the clutter taking up physical and mental space in your world and deciding what can go. Spend a day – preferably one full of thunder and lightning that even a nature lover can't go out in – being honest with yourself about what you really need. As the Japanese organising guru Marie Kondo suggests, if an item doesn't bring you joy, hold sentimental value or have a real use, get it out of your way. This season is all about making room for the fun, fresh and fabulous. Who knows, you might need to make room in your downstairs cupboard for a kayak this summer, so take your old printer and the scooter your kids have grown out of to a charity shop now. Sort out the pile of papers and shred what you don't need. Look at that pile of magazines and newspapers, and be honest with yourself about what you're really going to get around to reading and recycle the rest.

Wide open spaces – in your bedroom, on your desk, in your glove compartment – help you to get a wide, open mind, ready to be filled with new adventures. Encourage loved ones to do the same, especially if you share a home with them. If it isn't wanted, isn't needed or can't be fixed, get it out. This might sound like a bit of a chore, but once it's done it's done, and you'll have room and time in your life for those things that will truly make you grow, connect to the world and increase your well-being. No one ever regretted a good sort out.

Gather together your thoughts and things

Like a mother bird carefully weaving together all things strong, stable and beautiful to make a nest, you need to gather together the things you know will make your home more pleasurable this spring. I'm not talking just material items – I'm talking ideas, people, dreams and plans. Spring is the perfect time to sit down with a notepad and pen and think about what you want out and what you want in. Perhaps write a list of aims – five things you want to have achieved by summer, or five ways you want to feel better by next month. Perhaps you can write yourself a to-do list for your spring weekends (buying yourself fresh flowers every Friday, taking a walk every Saturday, visiting a new garden or stately home every Sunday).

Making lists works. It focuses the brain on what is truly important. You can also try writing a list of things you want to stop doing/thinking/worrying about, as a reminder that life is short and that you really don't need to check your social media every hour on the hour, or follow three soap operas, or do all your exercising indoors at the gym. Gather your dream life and ideal scenarios for spring on the page and watch them plant themselves in your reality.

Kate, 33

'People say this but rarely do it: stop and smell the roses. I always do, I love the old-fashioned, strong-smelling varieties, and I can't help but stop to sniff! Flowers have a true, pure beauty that can dazzle most of the senses if we remember to appreciate them. I adore spring-time blossom and how the pale pink variety makes the branches of trees look like they have candyfloss dripping from them. I love wading through a sea of bluebells, or tiptoeing across a carpet of lavender. When city life closes me off from life, a vase of flowers next to my bed or even the sight of a flower stall on a busy street reminds me of a million smells and sights.'

Catch spring fever

Spring is the perfect time to try new things and to push your-self, which is why it's the perfect season to start your own version of forest therapy and connecting more deeply with the natural world. You have decided to become a happier, less stressed, stronger you – not an unrecognisable you, just an updated, less anxious ver-sion, who might hug trees in your spare time. Well, I'm joking about the tree hugging (although it does feel good). Spring is about being brave and experimental, like all those animals you see in the forest, leaving their nests and flying for the first time or hopping away from their mothers. This is the season of accelerated glory, and you are your own best advocate.

Spring is the season to set yourself a list of once-in-a-lifetime experiences the natural world has to offer: moments you'd regret missing out on. These suggestions are from my own 'thank goodness I got around to doing that' list:

Take out a canoe or rowing boat for a water-world adventure. Dock along pretty banks to rest and check out the creatures that inhabit this aquatic area. When safely anchored, a picnic or a nap is a delight, the gentle rocking of the boat soothing for the body and mind. My children and godchildren persuaded me onto a boating lake in Suffolk last summer, and after my initial fear that I was in charge of five under-tens and capsizing would be terrible, we sang and floated, and worked our muscles as we drifted past ducks, and I will never forget how charming it was.

Cycle around a city – it's a good new way to take it all in and fall in love with it. Here's an example. New York can be a pretty heavy place in which to live, where zombies march on packed sidewalks staring into their handheld devices, get grimy on the subway or come to a smoggy standstill in taxi traffic. On Sundays when I first moved to Manhattan (and had no friends, whimper whimper), I'd hire a bike and cruise around Central Park and up to a pretty garden spot on a boating lake for lunch. This was how I got to know and admire the city. The aching thighs during Monday meetings (I'm not a natural athlete) were worth it.

Dance barefoot on a beach Kick off your shoes, your inhibitions and worries – and move. There's something freeing about the feel of sand between your toes. It not only exfoliates your soles but your soul too. And if you're thinking about shaking off winter overindulgences, know this: walking on sand burns 30 per cent more calories than walking on a flat human-made surface, so just imagine what dancing on sand would do. You don't have to wait until you're in St Barts either. Margate will do, Skegness, Barry Island. Just find some sand and groove.

Gaze up at the Northern Lights Notoriously fickle and good at hide and seek, this dazzling display cannot be kept to deadlines or diaries, but some tips will make your chances of catching the glorious Aurora Borealis late-night show more likely. Head to the auroral zone (Alaska, Canada, Sweden, Finland, Norway, Scotland and Iceland are top options) during winter or spring, when the nights are still dark but with less cloud cover. And, to avoid disappointment, in case they don't show, make sure you've gone to a place you'd love to see anyway – and try glacier hiking, husky sledging, mountain-pony trek-king or snowmobile racing.

Spring playlist

Get moving and grooving to these ten life-loving, energy-boosting tunes, perfect for this season of new hope and new beginnings – and more energy:

- 'Don't Stop' by Fleetwood Mac
- 'Spring is Here' by Frank Sinatra
- 'A Father's First Spring' by The Avett Brothers
- 'The First Day of Spring' by Noah and the Whale
- 'You're My Best Friend' by Queen
- 'Build Me Up Buttercup' by The Foundations
- 'Absolute Beginners' by David Bowie
- 'Wanna Be Startin' Somethin' by Michael Jackson
- 'Spring Haze' by Tori Amos
- 'Spring Manifestations' by Santana

Spring clean your soul

Your house and wardrobe are sorted, your suitcase is filled with aims and ambitions – what about your mind? This new season, the legendary time of renewal, is the perfect moment to ask yourself some deep and meaningful questions. Take a moment somewhere quiet, somewhere you can breathe deeply and be honest, and ask yourself these three questions:

1 Do I need to change any of the 'rules' my life has been governed by so far?

Do I need to always say yes to people and events? Do I need to bake everything from scratch? Do I need to throw dinner parties when I find them stressful and expensive? Without even realising it, we all fall into bad habits and time-costing restrictions. We spend time with people we don't adore, doing things that don't make our heart sing. Evaluate the 'rules' you've set out for yourself and change the ones you don't like. Rebel! Carve out a life that will make you happier this spring and for the seasons to come. Taking a good, honest look at how you're spending your time will help you to free up more time for the pursuits outlined in this book that will benefit you. I don't own an iron, for example. My mother is horrified, my mother-in-law is shocked, and I often wander about looking oddly crumpled. I don't care. Ironing is not a priority to me or to the happiness of my family; I'd rather spend time playing outdoors.

2 Do I need to lighten up and let go?

If, like me, you are kept awake at night by niggles and irks, and itchy-scratchy feelings of guilt or insecurity, you need to do an Elsa and let it go. Let's dump that mental weight like a heap of winter's snow, watch it melt and move forward guilt-free with a spring in our step. I hang on to things for too long, I always have since I was a child, and it's done me no favours whatsoever. I overanalyse everything and everyone, looking for signs that I've upset them or done them wrong. Freud would have had a field day and unearthed many a drama to explain my foibles away, but at some point – around turning 40 – I just gave up. An older, wiser friend told me two things around this time. First, you can't make people be like you; you just have to be able to like yourself. Secondly, you should leave any interaction with a friend or family member feeling warm and fuzzy. If you leave feeling upset or agitated, you need to address your attitude or distance yourself from their behaviour. Life is for living with love and lightness, not with dread or a cruel dredging up of the past. And life is too short not to spend your time feeling healthy, helpful and happy.

3 How can I stimulate my mind and body in new, refreshing ways?

Right, you've finished with all the self-analysis and looking backwards. Now, what can you do to put your best foot forward? How can you create this unleashed, free, happy you? Here are some ways to get there:

- **You can swap your toxic friends** (those embittered by jealousy, anger, aggression or extreme neediness towards you) for new ones whose interests align more closely to yours. Find them in a book club, a yoga studio, among mindful nature walkers, at your child's school gates, at an after-work social, at the local gardening club – anywhere you like being, anywhere that makes your life better. As you move forward into this new, exciting season, you will naturally attract like-minded people who are also aiming for the good things in life. Don't forget to bring your lovely old friends with you on these new journeys, too.

- **You can set up a competition** – with yourself, rather than being competitive with anyone else. Push yourself to be happier, healthier, more rested or better read. Set yourself challenges that will make you prosper and flourish as a person, and stop looking around at what other people are doing or what other people have.

- **Do something every day that scares you** – be it talking to a new person, going for a walk or a coffee on your own, starting to learn a new language or starting to grow herbs on your balcony when you are not renowned for your green fingers. The possibilities are endless and so, when you realise it, is your resourcefulness.

- **Find a mentor.** Be a mentor. Locate the people who will encourage you to seed positive ideas and want to watch them grow, and do the same for another – someone younger than you, or a few years behind you in your chosen field. We're all on this ladder of life together and it helps to pull each other up towards the sky.

- **Take on a physical challenge** and monitor your progress in a diary or journal. I'm not talking about taking part in Iron Man or wanting bulging biceps, but whatever fits into your lifestyle and desires – promise yourself five minutes of sun salutations every morning, a tree-lined walk every lunchtime, an outdoor swim every Sunday. Mental clarity and positivity benefit no end from physical movement.

Spring reads

Here are five books to rejuvenate you during a spring day
in a meadow:

- *The Secret Garden* by Frances Hodgson Burnett
- *On Beauty* by Zadie Smith
- *Enchanted April* by Elizabeth von Arnim
- *The Liar* by Stephen Fry
- *All Creatures Great and Small* by James Herriot

April showers bring spring flowers . . . and wellies

Of course, springtime isn't all about gambolling lambs, hopping bunnies and you wandering through dappled trees feeling
the year's first warmth on your skin while feeling blissfully
abundant; it can be pretty damp and drab
too. Some folks tend to use a downpour as
an excuse to hide in the dark and, of course,
there is a very real argument for keeping the
amount of sogginess in your life to a minimum. But, and it's a big *but*, cat-and-dog weather
also showers us with opportunities to feel alive
like no other weather system can. Why should
jumping in muddy puddles or catching rain-
drops on your tongue be the exclusive
privilege of the very young? I say the

older we get the more we need these kinds of innocent, stress-relieving pursuits.

I have always admired Gene Kelly grinning as he's getting a soaking in *Singin' in the Rain*. Next time there's a deluge, get out and recreate it (bar the run-in with a frosty policeman, please). Or you could find a semi-sheltered spot outdoors during a cloudburst (tin roofs are the best) and engage your senses, listening to the pitter-patter as it hits your hideout while watching the charcoal clouds push across your horizon. And, of course, a good day of window-washing will give you the chance to show off the cute wellington boots and matching anorak combo you've been desperate for an occasion to unleash. If all these pursuits fail to excite you, just remember that the forest – and your back garden – are drinking it all in, getting hydrated before summer beckons, and loving every drop.

Spring flowers

These blooms are abundant at this time of year and symbolic of the season, so treat your home – and yourself – to a posy if you can this spring:

- Daffodils
- Freesias
- Hyacinths
- Lily-of-the-valley
- Magnolias
- Peonies
- Tulips

Stephanie, 45

'I have observed late February to early March in Kentucky, where I live, a magic that happens every year in our rolling fields and hills. It is so subtle that I always wonder if others can see it. It is a shift in the hues of the terrain. The browns of winter reflect the colours of a dusky sky, then a purpling of the ground occurs, like a wash or a wave moving across it. Logically, I attribute it to spring, but I don't really know its source. Poetically, it is for me Earth's aura as it shifts to the coming season, and it beckons me to uncurl and twist gently from my own winter shell.'

MINDFULNESS MINUTE

Meditate on new beginnings and fresh starts, symbolic of spring. Close your eyes and think back to the person you were ten years ago. Who were you then? Now think about who you are today. Would the old you be proud and excited by your world today? What would make them proud? Give yourself a mental hug and congratulations for achieving so much. Now think forward. Who will you be in ten years' time? Set yourself some goals and imagine yourself blossoming and growing, reaching for the treetops like a bulb in the ground, bursting full of colour and life. Meditate on three things that you want to set in place. Now open your eyes and begin.

4

Summer Lovin'

'Summer afternoon – summer afternoon;
to me those have always been the two most
beautiful words in the English language.'

Henry James

Summer is the most sensuous of seasons. The temperature rises and clothes are abandoned. Sun-kissed skin and sun-bleached hair glows as the sun sets in a collage of reds and pinks across the sky. On long, balmy evenings the scent of jasmine lingers in the air, mingling with coconut-scented limbs and citrus drinks. Colours are more vibrant and people look happier. There is a rush of pina coladas and bikinis, lilos and gelato, flip-flops and mini golf, rock pools and pub gardens. This is the season that being outdoors was made for, when partying hard and chilling even harder is the order of the day. And, obviously, the restorative power of a snooze in the shade of a tree as a warm breeze swirls around you should never be underestimated. Summer is simply the season of sumptuous delight, when even Mother Nature takes a holiday to sit back and admire her good work.

Science and reason of the summer season

The horror stories of the warmer months – wasps' nests, mosquito bites, lobster-red sunburn, hair-destroying humidity – can be avoided (or ignored) with due care and diligence, and should certainly not stop you from making the most of getting outside and benefitting from the natural plus points of the hottest months. Why?

- Studies (and our own experience) show that we eat better – naturally and easily – in summer. The abundance of tempting fresh fruit, salad and vegetables is high in vitamin C and antioxidants but low in fat and pointless calories. We're also more likely to drink our recommended two litres of water a day in warm weather, which helps to flush out toxins and improve digestion.
- Ultraviolet light converts dangerous cholesterol to vitamin D, so getting out in the sun's bright rays for ten minutes every day is a good way of lowering cholesterol, which in turn will lower the risk of heart disease and stroke.
- A rise in temperature lowers the risk of deep-vein thrombosis as warm weather helps blood vessels

enlarge, allowing for improved blood circulation.
- Warm weather eases the aches and pains of arthritis, allowing sufferers to feel more agile and supple.
- Clear, sunny days also reduce the chances of an onset of an attack for migraine sufferers.
- People are less likely to die from a heart attack in the summer, a UK study of 11,000 people showed. Scientists believe higher levels of vitamin D play a protective part in shielding those who suffer with heart problems, and also improves their chance of survival.
- Warm nights inspire people to lose the flannel pyjamas and sleep naked. And this is good if you share a bed with someone you love, because skin-on-skin time increases oxytocin, making you feel all loved and cosy, which will lead to more sex, which has lots of physical and mental benefits of its own when done right.
- You sweat more. That might sound awful, but a good perspiration session really is an excellent way of opening your pores and getting rid of bacteria and toxins, which improves the look of your skin. More sweat also means more pheromones, the body's natural scent that makes someone irresistible.

Friluftsliv-on-sea: the benefits of water therapy

Water works. It really does, in a myriad of ways. Our bodies are made up of 60 per cent water (our brains 75 per cent!) so it makes sense that we should learn to love it. Slurp it, look at it, sit in it – which are all easier to do in summer when the weather is warmer and the days are longer. How can you get into a routine of upping your aqua this season so that it becomes second nature throughout the year?

1 Drink it

Start your day the water way. Wake up with a glass of water, before you eat or drink anything else. This simple, free daily task will rehydrate the body and restore the fluids used up overnight. Doing this will help in transporting nutrients through the body, maintaining the correct body temperature, digesting food and washing the brain with essential electrical energy. A single glass can speed up the brain's processing and creative power, improve memory and help us to focus. Research shows that drinking 475ml of cold water first thing boosts a person's metabolism by up to 24 per cent, so staying hydrated can help you shift excess pounds too. Another thing, water is the great beautifier! Dehydration is one of the biggest causes for that dry, crinkled and wrinkled look we face as we get older, so irrigating your epidermis with Adam's ale will plump you up and return your youthful glow.

Health guidelines recommend that men drink 3 litres of fluid per day, and women drink 2.2 litres (this can include other drinks too, but not caffeinated or alcoholic ones, which dehydrate the body), and yet a survey by the Centers for Disease Control and Prevention in the US highlighted how up to 50 per cent of the US population were not meeting this suggestion, and we Brits are guilty of under-supping, too, a problem which a *British Journal of Nutrition* study says leaves us foggy headed.

Make sure you are not one of those people. Water will make you brighter, lighter with better working bowels and fewer headaches – seriously. I remember to start my day like this by leaving the right-sized glass next to the kettle, and make myself down a full glass before I treat myself to my morning coffee. Some friends drink it warm with a slice of lemon – the citrus adding a morning burst of vitamin C that can be easily absorbed into the body before it fills up with other stuff – but I prefer cold and plain. Either is better than nothing. Buy a filter so that you always have tasty, cool water on tap – add a few slices of cucumber or orange if you find the taste too dull. Even getting your litres in with water mixed with a fruit cordial is better than not drinking any.

Staying alive, staying hydrated

In the hotter summer months, drinking water regularly is crucial, especially when you're outside, walking or exercising. Carry a water bottle with you, and keep one on your desk at work. You can also sip on mugs of herbal tea in the evening to help you unwind and keep your fluids up. Eat foods full of water such as salad, fruit and vegetables. And remember, often feelings of hunger are just feelings of thirst – drink before you eat to see if that sates your appetite. Physically, you'll feel it if you're dehydrated. If your lips are dry, drink. If your wee is dark yellow with a strong scent, drink.

Home hydration

Pour two cups of Epsom salts into your home tub for a relaxing soak that promises to soothe aches and pains, ease overworked muscles and rehydrate the skin. I always add a few drops of lavender essential oil to my bath to up the stress-relieving experience. Adding sea kelp powder to your soak will draw out impurities and toxins, which could help your health, too. After taking a dip in the Dead Sea a few years ago, I also occasionally treat myself to bath treatments from that region too, the goodness bottled up and shipped to my front door.

2 Exercise in it

It's all going swimmingly. Taking the plunge will only improve your life. Swimming is the ideal way to exercise for all fitness levels and ages, because it is gentle on joints while giving your heart and lungs a great aerobic workout. The water resistance builds muscle and lowers blood pressure. You can burn the most calories doing fast crawl or butterfly stroke, but any stroke will offer a good, all round body challenge. Swimming in warm water has been proven to ease stiffness and pain, and increase flexibility by reducing the load on joints, which is specifically useful for pregnant women, the overweight or those with arthritis.

Hydrotherapy, as swimming or floating in water is known, also has a calming effect on the mind, the weightlessness of water offering a physical and mental distraction from the weight of life's worries. The breathing patterns that you fall into during a swim regulate brain waves, which also quietens the interior chatter that leads to anxiety.

Swimming in the sea has its own name – it's that special: thalassotherapy (a word first used by the god of all things good for us, Hippocrates, no less). Ocean water is swimming in minerals including sodium, chloride, sulphate, calcium and magnesium – all helpful healers of skin conditions such as psoriasis and eczema. Swimming in the sea is also known to reduce the symptoms of hay fever and respiratory issues; one reason suggested for this is that the saline splashing reduces inflammation in the nose and throat. Seawater is also brimming with microorganisms that produce antibiotic and antibacterial immunity boosters in humans. So, let's ride that wave, shall we?

Ice, ice baby

If you're brave enough, a dip in an icy cold lake, river, natural mineral bath or ocean activates temperature receptors under the skin that release endorphins, serotonin and cortisol – so the feel-good benefits flood in (although always think of your own safety and stay away from danger). If you're not feeling the freeze, no fear. Swimming or bathing in warm seawater increases circulation, restoring essential minerals that have been drowned out of you by stress, poor diet and other modern-living poisons.

3 Look at it

An ocean view is worth more than its weight in water!

It won't come as a surprise to most of us that new research has indicated living near the coast has powerful, positive impacts on a person's health. Who hasn't spent some time staring at the ocean and fallen into a meditative state, feeling stresses and knots flowing away with the tide? There is now scientific proof showing that staring at the sea changes our brain waves and that the colour blue is associated psychologically with feelings of peace and calm. All this while the rhythmic ebb and flow of the tide de-stimulates our overactive, overtired brains. This wave of oceanic love – the sights, sounds (and let's not forget the smell) activates something called our parasympathetic nervous system, the part of us that is responsible for helping us to chill out and release the worries. So just looking at it – not even drinking or swimming in it, just sitting near to it – gives us a major health boost.

Summer Reads

Here are five dazzling books to drift off with during a sunny summer's day on the beach:

- *On Chesil Beach* by Ian McEwan
- *Wide Sargasso Sea* by Jean Rhys
- *Lace* by Shirley Conran
- *Valley of the Dolls* by Jacqueline Susann
- *Brighton Rock* by Graham Greene

4 Breathe it

Vitamin sea – that salty, briny air we have loved to suck down in lungfuls for centuries – we might like it so much because an ocean breeze is filled with negative ions. The *Journal of Alternative Complementary Medicine* thinks that negative ion therapy – yes, the posh name for breathing in sea air – helps to treat the symptoms of SAD, like depression and anxiety. Ocean air is also said to thin mucus, improve lung function, reduce coughing and decrease sinus pressure in patients with lung disease, highlighting the power of the playa for us all. Sea air is so good for our health because it contains minute droplets of seawater (which, as we know, is filled with lots of good stuff) and is largely free from the harmful vapours of everyday life such as soot particles and exhaust fumes. So, even if you don't live on the coast, try to take regular trips for a bracing walk and a few deep breaths.

Summer playlist

Get moving and grooving to these ten sun-soaking, sea-splashing tunes, perfect for this season of hot nights and bright days – and more fun:

- 'Pocketful of Sunshine' by Natasha Bedingfield
- 'Cheerleader' by OMI
- 'La Isla Bonita' by Madonna
- 'Strawberry Swing' by Coldplay
- 'California Gurls' by Katy Perry featuring Snoop Dogg
- 'Wouldn't it be Nice' by The Beach Boys
- 'Soak Up the Sun' by Sheryl Crow
- 'Walking on Sunshine' by Katrina and The Waves
- 'Steal My Sunshine' by Len
- 'English Summer Rain' by Placebo

Andrea, 41

'You can't beat a beach hut. They're picture-perfect inside and out; every time I take a photo of our one it looks like it could be a postcard. Our hut is also the one place where I have no service on my phone, so I can't check it all day long, which is such a relief in this day and age where we are on our phones 24/7. My kids get 100 per cent of my attention, and if they're napping or playing happily on their own, I may even get to read the paper or a magazine, or just sit and daydream as I listen to and look at the sea. It's a true, rare treat.'

Beauty and the beach

It's a shore thing. Nothing says escapism like a trip to the coast. The quiet contemplation of collecting shells and driftwood, the mindful search for crabs and coral. A summer's day at the seaside is at once the most natural thing in the world and the most luxurious, associated with childhood holidays and good times with friends, the warm feeling of happy nostalgia it prompts in us is worth the journey alone. Surrounded by centillions of grains of sand promotes a proper sense of perspective as well. Clutch a handful and watch it slip away. There are many life lessons in that one movement: life is fleeting, life is beautiful; enjoy the simple things in life; be patient.

There are recognised physical benefits to getting sandy, too:

- In Egypt 'sand baths' are a thing. People who are aching and exhausted are buried up to their necks in sand for 15 minutes to feel the healing powers of the heavy, hot sand, which they believe will relieve the symptoms of rheumatism and joint pain, while they get a soothing head massage. Why not get your kids to give you a sand bath next time you're at the seaside? Just remember to keep your neck, head and hands free, sticking out from the sand, above burial level.

- Sand offers a great, natural – and free – exfoliating treatment for the hands, feet and body, softening the skin and removing dead skin cells. Take a dip, then rub yourself gently with sand; now return to the sea to swim yourself clean. Or take a cup of sand home to mix with your daily body moisturiser or almond oil. Smooth sand mixed with moisturiser over your body first, then jump in the shower and rub with circular movements as water lightly rinses your skin. Rinse after a couple of minutes and feel the difference. You're a smooth operator.

- Walking on sand works your muscles in a different way from walking on sturdy surfaces, giving you a unique stretch. Walking on the sand will also give you a free reflexology session. The shifting sand underfoot works on various pressure points, releasing toxins and tension with every sandy step.

- Running on a beach is like taking on a natural assault course: it tests your agility as you leap over driftwood and accelerate over the incoming tide, and it gets your heart racing in a unique way.

- Even lying on sand helps. A careful sunbathing session exposing the right amount of sun (15 minutes before applying sunscreen, see page 29) to your skin without damaging it will push the endocrine system to secrete endorphins, which – combined with the soothing sur-roundings – could chill you out more than a trip to an expensive spa.

- Going barefoot on the sand is great for grounding, also known as 'earthing'. This practice is a way of removing excess positive electrons, which build up over time during stressful modern life, by stamping them into the ground, which has a mild negative charge to it, and thus rebalancing us to a healthy neutral state. And walking barefoot outdoors just feels nice, connecting us to the natural world with our bare skin. Going barefoot also gives us a chance to realign our posture, which gets unbalanced pounding the pavement in shoes.

How to embrace nature during a summer city break

It's very easy to get your nature fix if you're heading to a beach resort or to a mountain cabin for your summer holiday, but city breaks will take more planning. Before you leave, follow nature blogs in the area where you're travelling to, or check out the location using hashtags on social media and make a note of any restaurants, coffee shops and bars that have picturesque outdoor areas to relax in. Ask friends who have been before for picnic and park ideas. Buy a guide book and see which museums, castles and cathedrals have gardens for you to explore. See if any artificial beaches or boating lakes have sprung up in the city. If you are in the UK, are there any gardens open to the public through the National Garden Scheme, as well as larger gardens you can visit? You might also find open-air yoga classes or nature mindfulness walks offered in some cities. And don't get stuck in the city limits with the city's limitations: take public transport (a fun experience all of its own, especially in a different country) out into the suburbs and beyond, exploring nearby vineyards, farms, parks, rivers and country retreats.

Checking out sports in the area is a good way of trying new things and getting a fun dose of the outdoors too, so check local listings when you arrive for big games and shows.

Staycation spice-up!

Even if you're not flying off to some exotic locale this summer, you can bring excitement into your nature-loving routine by trying some new sports or pastimes. How about trying some of the following?

- A walk in that botanical garden you've never done to get ideas for your own green space.
- A game of tennis at the local courts with willing friends. It's a good excuse for a refreshing Pimm's, if ever I knew one.
- A kayak at a nearby water centre, lake or river.
- A game of volleyball – it's what the beautiful people are doing these days.
- A game of boules, bocce or petanque. You can take your own set somewhere fun or take advantage of the trend

in pub gardens having their own flat, open space for a game.

- An outdoor movie, or you could buy or hire a projector to host your own. Don't forget the popcorn.
- An afternoon picking strawberries at a local patch.
- New foods at the local farmers' market.
- Set up your own ice cream parlour – complete with edible glitter and rainbow sprinkles and vintage glass bowls – as a fun feast for friends or family.
- A swing and sleep in a hammock in your garden.
- An outdoor concert – head out for a head bang with a picnic.
- A game of Lawn Twister – spray paint different-coloured circles onto your back lawn and get bendy.
- A glow-in-the-dark disco in your back garden – get all eighties with luminous glow sticks, necklaces and flashing deely boppers.

Anna, 30

'My French neighbour sprinkles her front garden path with dried lavender buds when she is preparing for a summer party. As her guests start to arrive on warm sunlit evenings, the flowers get trodden underfoot, and the most beautiful, pungent smell fills her garden.'

Summer flowers

These blooms are abundant at this time of year and symbolic of the season, so treat your home – and yourself – to a posy if you can this summer:

- Cornflowers
- Dahlias
- Delphiniums
- Larkspurs
- Lavender
- Lilies
- Night-scented stocks
- Roses
- Sweet peas
- Tuberose

Until next summer

That boat trip, that barbecue, the game of baseball in the park, seaside smiles and sunset climbs, the sand dollar you hold on to as a keepsake of a summer well spent – magic memories seem to be made all the more readily during the warmest season. We are at our best, it seems, when the sun is shining and we are out and about exploring the world. Far from being maudlin or self-indulgent, looking back nostalgically on the summer just gone, or a summer from your childhood, can increase your sense of well-being. Recalling special moments with friends and family can make us feel connected to the world and raise our self-esteem, as researchers at the University of Southampton have discovered. Triggering such happy memories can ease depression and make us feel more optimistic about the future. And thinking back on good times tends to give us an attitude of gratitude, which in turn persuades us to be more kind and loving.

How can you hold on to the feelings of summer as we drift towards darker, drearier days?

- **Don't let photos die on Facebook** or on your phone – print them out, or choose your 12 favourites and have them made into a calendar for the next year. Do it soon. You think you'll remember and make reminiscing a priority during the hibernating months of winter, but you won't. Do it while the memories are hot.
- **Set your song of the summer** as your ringtone or your morning alarm.
- **Going forward during meditation**, imagine yourself in the place you felt the most alive and content this summer: that undiscovered cove you stumbled on by accident, or the flower show you visited on the bank holiday weekend. Recall the sights, smells and sounds, and let nostalgia wash over you. Wait for the smile to creep across your face and your heart.

- **Forget about being generic** and counting sheep on a restless autumn night: count the umbrellas in your mojitos or the bumble bees in your flowerbed you got to experience this summer.
- **Re-read a book you enjoyed** on holiday. My mum makes a point of writing where she was and when on the inside jacket of every memorable book she reads, and the real-life moments surrounding the fictional ones come flooding back whenever she opens it again.
- **Buy a piece of art** or a print of a place that means a great deal to you. Just looking at a beach, the mountains or a forest view you love decreases anxiety, so placing a painting somewhere you see every day will help in a multitude of ways.
- **Make a scrapbook** of all the tickets, passes, notes and Polaroids of the summer and keep them out as a coffee-table book to dip into in quiet, reflective moments.

MINDFULNESS MINUTE

Sit by the sea and close your eyes. Relax each muscle and soften your face to the rhythmic swirl of the waves. In. Out. In. Out. Breathe the sea air deeply and fully. Rock on your haunches slowly, mimicking the push and pull of the tide. Now open your eyes and focus on the majesty of the body of water you are sitting beside – the depth, the colour, the strength, the beauty, the sparkle – and imagine letting all those qualities wash over you.

5

Fall in Love

'Is not this a true autumn day? Just the still melancholy
that I love – that makes life and nature harmonise. The birds
are consulting about their migrations, the trees are putting on
the hectic or the pallid hues of decay, and begin to strew the
ground, that one's very footsteps may not disturb the repose
of earth and air, while they give us a scent that is a perfect
anodyne to the restless spirit. Delicious autumn! My very soul
is wedded to it, and if I were a bird I would fly about
the earth seeking the successive autumns.'

George Eliot

Autumn, or fall as it is known in the US, is the season when the
world mellows out and takes stock on what has already been
achieved. Change occurs, but at a reassuringly slow drift rather
than a hurried panic. Planet Earth takes on a warm glow as the
sun shrinks back into the soil. Golden moments with friends,
family and self shape the months leading up to the festive

season. The nights stretch out once more, lit by bonfires and fireworks, log fires and sparklers. There are rustling leaves and crunchy pathways, conkers and acorns, brandy snaps, apple bobbing and pumpkin picking. Keats famously described autumn as the 'season of mists and mellow fruitfulness', and our routines reflect Mother Nature's chilled-out, contented vibe too.

Ode to autumn

Autumn is owed great respect for being awesomely good for us in a number of ways. Here are seven reasons to make the most of this season:

1 When the clocks go back and mornings become darker and cooler, we're naturally more likely to get some extra shut-eye. Autumn offers the perfect antidote to the restlessness of summer sleep, as the lack of light and a drop in temperature makes it better quality (research says the ideal temp for sleeping is between 15°C and 20°C.). No sweaty tangling in the bed sheets or annoying whirr of the air-conditioning unit. And good sleep makes everyone feel invincible.

2 Seasonal superfoods are abundant, nutritious, delicious and easy to prepare: stews, soups and casseroles warm and satisfy every day, filled to brimming with reasonably priced squash, pumpkin, sweet potatoes and all manner of seasonal root vegetables. Beta-carotene, the fab food compound found with no effort in autumn, helps to prevent certain cancers, heart disease and high blood pressure. A portion of pumpkin weighing 225g offers a crazy amount of vitamin A – 200 per cent of your daily recommendation – and a hearty wallop of vitamin E, which provides crucial goodness for healthy skin, teeth and vision. Also, roast up some parsnips for a feast of immune-boosting vitamin C.

3 You can celebrate those back-to-school vibes and get down with some books and learning. Geek has never felt so chic. The autumn is the perfect time to start a new hobby or habit, such as joining a book club, starting to learn a new language or taking an evening class in local history. And this is the perfect season to take these habits outside, without the fear of being bitten or burnt.

4 Brisk autumn weather doesn't just feel good on your skin and in your lungs, a study shows that cold and crisp weather benefits your mind too. Researchers split a group into two and gave them both a memorisation test, half on a sunny, warm day typical of summer, the other on a cooler, cloudy day typical of autumn – and the cooler group had much better luck at remembering things.

5 This is the perfect season to set new outdoor goals that you can keep, or to revisit old ones that have been lost over the previous few months. The decadence of summer and its overindulgences – late nights, lie-ins and travel, not to mention eating and drinking too much – are over, and a new air of restoration and good sense abounds. Take another look at your goals from spring, check in on them and your mental and physical well-being, and get back into a rhythm. Commit to the weekly forest walk, nurturing your windowsill herb garden or morning meditations.

6 You'll start fancying hot drinks again after a summer off. Green and black teas are steeped in antioxidants that help to keep flu at bay during the cooler months, so sip away.

7 The mane event will be your crowning glory The humidity of summer has subsided and the too-dry indoor temperatures of winter are in the future, so your hair is looking and feeling good when you're out and about.

Potent pumpkin

Autumn is the time to pick it, eat it, drink it, carve it and light it, but that isn't all a pumpkin can do to spice up your life. According to research at Chicago's Smell and Taste Treatment and Research Center, the smell of pumpkin turns men wild with desire. Mixed with lavender, the scent increases penile blood flow in participants by an average of 40 per cent. Pumpkins are also rich in zinc, which increases testosterone. Combine these natural fragrances with the cooler, cosier nights and, well, things can get pretty romantic on that twilight stroll. My, oh pie!

Turn over a new leaf

The ethereal blanketing of the earth with leaves every autumn is nothing short of soul lifting. The amber richness of the shed leaves softens the world and slows our pace. Experiencing such beauty doesn't just feel lovely, it's lovely for our brain, too. Walking among the plum tones and orange shades, and engaging with the season's changing prettiness, activates the brain's medial orbitofrontal cortex, which helps with sharp thinking and deep relaxation. The colours red and yellow are recognised as stimulating shades, giving your eyes – and then your whole being – a boost, so expect even a quick lunchtime dash through the park to pick up your mood.

The contrast that occurs in early autumn – green against red, yellow versus brown – grabs our attention and excites our brain, making a bright, engaging change from the solid greens of a spring and summer forest. It gives us a unique visual stimulus. We forget our daily worries and fears, overwhelmed by the beauty of nature – even if just for the duration of a walk or a relaxation session outside. The trees and their daily change also give us a good chance to practise mindfulness. How many leaves have dropped since I was last here? What colour strikes me the most? When we encounter the largesse of life like this, we are humbled into forgetting our self-centred niggles and look outward to appreciate the world.

Autumn playlist

Get moving and grooving to these ten cosy-comforting, laid-back loving tunes, perfect for this season of change and chilling – and saying goodbye to summer:

- 'The Boys of Summer' by Don Henley
- 'Endless Summer Nights' by Richard Marx
- 'November Rain' by Guns N' Roses
- 'When the Leaves Come Falling Down' by Van Morrison
- 'Pale September' by Fiona Apple
- 'Can't Help Falling in Love with You' by UB40
- 'The Boys of Fall' by Kenny Chesney
- 'Skyfall' by Adele
- 'Wake Me Up When September Ends' by Green Day
- 'Harvest Moon' by Neil Young

Autumn workouts

This isn't just the most gorgeous season, it can be the best for exercise outside too. The sun is still shining in early autumn, but not so ferociously; the crispness in the air invigorates without overheating us. Try these outdoor activities that build happy memories and muscle:

- Scrumping for apples can burn up to 300 calories in a few hours.
- A forest trail has never been so resplendent for walking along. As you march through the fantastic foliage watch out for the busy squirrels preparing for frost by gathering acorns and nuts.
- Choosing pumpkins and lugging them home is good for building arm muscles.
- Blackberry picking is great for flexibility, and offers a flavonoid boost from the end of summer to early autumn.
- Raking leaves gives a good cardiovascular workout and burns approximately 50 calories per 30 minutes.
- Dancing the can-can in a forest of fallen leaves is a good way to kick-start your metabolism.
- As the kids are heading back to school, relive your childhood and go back to the outdoor games and challenges you had as a child in the playground. Hopscotch, skipping rope, playing catch. Dare I mention cross-country running, the bane of my teen years? I hated it, but some friends adored it. If that was you, pick it up again. Another way to get some outdoor exercise in is to sign up to help or coach all the new teams that start up around this time of the year at your children's schools or to commit to walking the kids to school rather than driving or putting them on a bus. These morning

walks – if not madly rushed – can be a great way for you and your child to set affirmations for the day ahead and to observe the changing world around you. No season surpasses autumn for the daily adjustments to nature.

Dark force

The nights are drawing in, but that is no excuse to take your fitness routine inside or to disengage with the natural world, just be safe. If you're out walking, wear a reflective vest and carry a flashlight. If you're cycling, affix a light to your bicycle and helmet.

Fall into a regular family and friends' routine

There is a natural pull at this time of the year to start shrinking back into our homes and our bones, and to wrap up in brick walls in front of the television. But there are a few fun seasonal events that not only force us to be social but also to be outdoors. Make the most of these gatherings, because time spent with family and friends has proven benefits to our mental and physical health. Bonfire Night is one of them, of course, where familial connections (or a stuffed effigy of a 17th-century political rebel) are re-lit and you realise how great it is to spend time with people with whom you get on like a house on fire. (I'll also be talking more about Bonfire Night later.)

Family time

The biggest plus of outdoor family autumn experiences is that it forces you all to unplug, to step away from this mind-numbing, anxiety-swelling technology-obsessed road we're on and to reconnect, in person, with real people. Bonding, warm apple cider in one hand, jacket potato in the other, as you create strong memories with people you love, puts you in a good mood and decreases stress.

Studies show that families who enjoy everyday activities together – not just expensive holidays and big events – have strong emotional ties that allow them to adapt better to new or difficult situations. And it pays forward. Children who have happy family memories from their youth are more likely to make the effort to recreate that environment when they become parents. A weekly autumnal stroll along a forest trail, sharing your news of the week, could forge great bonds all year round – and for the next generation. Environmental scientists believe quality time spent outdoors, away from the bombardment of manufactured distractions we are faced with indoors, increases our attention span and reduces ADHD in children. What a great way for kids to start the school year. Family time also builds self-esteem in children. When young-sters feel that they are valued by their parents and extended family, they feel positive about themselves and therefore find it easier to build strong relationships in their friendship circles too.

Friend time

Friends are the family we choose ourselves, and the right ones can become everything to us in good times and bad. But several recent studies show that the number of friends we have is falling, as the amount of time spent outdoors is falling. There's a correlation here. We're indoors on social media, leading these weirdly public yet closed-off lives, forgetting what really gets our endorphins flowing: an active, outdoor social life with people we adore. We have to get outside and get out of this rut, people. Because studies show that there are so many benefits to comradeship.

Friends extend your life, in fact research uncovered that the effect of strong social ties has twice as strong an impact on your lifespan as exercising and was the equivalent of quitting smoking. Friends give free stress relief in the form of the 'talking cure': we get to unburden ourselves and talk things through with people we trust. Friends keep your brain sharp, as we age: studies have found a link between an absence of social attachments and cognitive decline. Friends help us to get through tough times of rejection and upset. The stress hormone cortisol is lessened in people who feel that they have the support of close friends during times of trauma. After the distractions and travel of summer, autumn is the perfect time to get back together with your chosen people.

Autumn reads

Here are five books to thrill – and spook – you during an autumn day in the forest:

- *The Remains of the Day* by Kazuo Ishiguro
- *Northanger Abbey* by Jane Austen
- *The Turn of the Screw* by Henry James
- *Harry Potter and the Philosopher's Stone* by J.K. Rowling
- *The Secret History* by Donna Tartt

Spooktacular season

Halloween may be associated with ghosts, ghouls and a gruesomely gross amount of sugary sweets, but it's not all scary stuff. Halloween gives everyone an excuse to get outside, meet the neighbours, embrace the chill of a brisk autumn evening and be creative. You get to use your imagination, dress up, revert to the careless excitement of your youth and decorate the front of your house with cobwebs, orange fairy lights and petrified looking black cats. If you have children, you get to partake in the coolest family fiesta ever: trick or treating, probably the easiest time of the year to get the kids outside, away from a screen, and walking the neighbourhood with you. Well, there is the promise of chocolate in it!

And of course, there are pumpkin Jack-o-lanterns, which

don't only provide mental stimulation while carving them, but a nutritional power boost from the discarded pulp inside. So don't throw the good stuff away. You already know about the glorious levels of beta-carotene, vitamins A and C from the flesh – but the seeds are fab too, packed full of protein, magnesium, potassium and zinc. Studies show that these tiny tasty treats can help to prevent depression. No trick. And don't forget that other Halloween superfood: garlic. Not only will it keep vampires at bay, but it is also packed full of vitamins, and it will help to scare away any autumnal colds too.

And finally, what Halloween is really about: finding the fun in being frightened, which researchers are now declaring to be good for us. Being scared in an exciting, non-threatening Halloween kind of way (taking a ghost tour or walking around a haunted house at a funfair, for example) ramps up adrenalin and dopamine, flooding our muscles with oxygen as we prepare for fight or flight, albeit fake! Because it is Halloween, and the scary-looking thing at the end of your road is your neighbour wearing his bed sheet, you get to enjoy the pumped-up and giddy feeling, rather than it being bad for you. And after the rush of chemicals, your body feels deeply relaxed.

Claire, 42

'The kids and I love to go wandering in the woods near our home – especially in the autumn when the ground becomes a soft blanket of colour. The girls and I make homes for the fairies and play parks for them out of crispy bark and golden leaves, and anything else we find. A feather is always a good find. It turns a walk in the woods into something more magical and exciting for them, and their imaginations can run wild. We bought Freddie, my ten-year-old son, a simple Swiss Army knife and he loves to search for sticks that he can whittle into various shapes: an arrow, a gnome, a totem pole ...'

Relight my fire

Guy Fawkes Night (or Bonfire Night) gives us another chance to meet our neighbours and hang out with friends and family. And it has to take place outside because – fireworks. You may lose your dignity while bobbing for apples, but you'll win laughs. And there are sparklers! Sparklers turn us all into whirling, twirling five-year-olds, getting arty in the night sky, writing our names and drawing hearts. And after the oohs and ahhs have erupted from the gathered, chilly crowd, a peaceful quiet descends. There is nothing finer than mingling around the bonfire, rosy-cheeked and mittened, listening to the crackling logs burn as red sparks fly up into a starlit black sky. For the desire to be outside on a chilly November night with friends, taking in the sights and sounds of the night alone, this very British festival is a winner.

Gratitude attitude

Thanksgiving is, of course, an American celebration, a secular blessing for the harvest and the previous year, a time to eat too much, sit too much and watch too much sport. After living in America for 12 years I've really started to love it. It truly is the US version of Christmas (Turkey! Stuffing! Weird uncles!) with a beautiful question at the heart of it: what are you thankful for?

The first Thanksgiving dinner I ever went to was in New York City with a hodgepodge group of Americans and immigrants, and a handful of British ex-pats. As we sat at the table in front of the gluttonous feast, the Americans led us in a sharing circle. We each spoke about a moment or a person that had meant a great deal to us that year, and then we retuned to the present and thanked the host, the friends and the day. I got teary – more than that really, as new and old friends bravely and humorously shared their highlights and saviours. Since then, every Thanksgiving, in a group or on my own, I've taken the time to muse on what I have to be grateful for.

Being thankful is an important position from which to look at the world. We are too easily persuaded that we have it tough, or certainly tougher than the luck-finding, jammy friends or siblings we seem to be faced with on a daily basis. The act of looking and acknowledging our own good fortune – in conversations, in a diary, or in our own daily affirmations – can have many social, mental and physical benefits.

Socially, being polite and showing how grateful you are to have someone in your life is beneficial. A study published in the journal *Emotion* showed how acknowledging people's contribution to your world, by thanking them in person, or by note, or just by your behaviour towards them, will make you more likeable and popular. That means you have more friends to meet for forest trail walks.

Mentally, an attitude of gratitude reduces the amount of time we get weighed down and worried by the toxic emotions of jealousy, frustration and regret. When you're feeling grateful, you can't help but feel uplifted, and your self-esteem is less battered by what other people are achieving or receiving around you, as you focus on your own game. Feeling thankful for one's own position also makes us more empathetic to others who are not quite so fortunate.

Studies have found that people who feel grateful for life take better care of their physical health. They feel lucky, but they don't want to push that luck, so they exercise regularly and go for regular check-ups with their doctors.

A study in *Applied Psychology: Health and Wellbeing* journal revealed that writing down a few positive sentiments before going to bed helped people sleep deeper and longer as well – another massive health hit.

Autumn flowers

These blooms are abundant at this time of the year and symbolic of the season, so treat your home – and yourself – to a posy if you can this autumn:

- Aster
- Autumn-flowering clematis
- Chrysanthemums
- Hydrangea

Kate, 30

'Growing up, I lived near a lake and would find myself out there most days, whether I was swimming or fishing or taking out the rowing boat. The lake during the summer was fun and exciting, but the lake in the autumn was always my favourite. I can remember long walks I would take around the lake, with the leaves changing from green to yellow to red to brown and then falling. I can remember the quiet at night when no one was there: a serene and peaceful experience that always made me feel more whole. Looking back on my childhood, the lake during the autumn was my way of escaping and enjoying the ever-changing beauty of nature. The crisp air would reinvigorate me, and the surrounding scenery would lift my spirits – as it still does to this day whenever I return home.'

MINDFULNESS MINUTE

Get comfortable outdoors somewhere, on a soft bed of leaves preferably, close your eyes and sink your body into the earth. Imagine – or perhaps feel in real life – leaves falling from the trees and covering you with the lightest touches. Imagine their gentle sway to and fro, the seesawing of the different warm shades. Orange, gold, brown, red. As the leaves fall to the ground and rest, feel yourself enter a restful state.

6

Winter Wonderland

'I wonder if the snow loves the trees and fields, that it kisses them so gently? And then it covers them up snug, you know, with a white quilt; and perhaps it says, "Go to sleep, darlings, till the summer comes again."'

Lewis Carroll

Snow flurries and snow crystals, parties and pantomimes, classic movies and cheesy music, wrapping up presents and wrapping up warm, silly games and streamers. Winter is the time of fairy tales. Mother Nature paints herself in glitter and welcomes in the mythical creatures of the season, while hibernating animals hole up in her warm ground and cosy tree trunks.

I remember as a child, watching my smoky breath unfurl in the chilly morning air on my walk to school, pretending to ice skate across the shimmering pavement as the bare branches overhead twinkled with icicles. My eyeballs were dazzled by the festive beauty of it all, the lustre of frozen pearls turning my world into a life-sized snow globe. Winter is truly the season that Mother Nature becomes a Hollywood screen siren, the globe her sound stage. Loving her moment in the spotlight, the great outdoors becomes the bedazzling location for all that glistens and gleams. To hide indoors would mean missing out.

Winter is snow excuse to stay indoors!

You may be wanting to get *hygge*-y with it, because – brrrrrr! – frostbite, but you'd be missing out on the magic and sparkle, and feel-good benefits, of bracing the cold and stepping out into the brittle air of this season. Things like:

- Exposure to cold weather will increase your energy for hours afterwards. Just a short walk outside at lunchtime will keep your inner oil fires burning through an afternoon of work or parenting. And I'm not just talking about physical energy. Cold temperatures boost decision-making abilities too.
- You can breathe better when it's brisk outside. The crisp, clean air of Christmastime means lower ozone levels and better air quality.
- For children, winter weather allows them to stretch their brains and different muscles. They get to play and create in new ways: igloos, snowball fights, snow angels, snowmen – and move their bodies in different directions, pulling their friends on a sledge or pushing their way through sleet and slush. These new weather dilemmas also make them use their problem-solving muscles:

how not to slip over on the ice, how does mum defrost the windscreen, how do I climb a snowy hill? The ever-changing environment of wintertime provides constant creative challenges and stimulations.

- Getting children – and you! – outside every day will help you to avoid some of the bacteria and viruses that can thrive in a home once the heating has to be turned on. It's harder to pass germs to each other in cold, fresh air.

- Pesky creatures thrive in warm climates, so expect a total lockdown on annoying mosquitoes, midges, ticks and bugs as the temperature drops.

- If you've ever put ice on an injury, you will know that cold temperatures reduce inflammation and swelling. So, think of winter as one giant ice pack, reducing pain and swelling all over your body. Cryotherapy – a therapy where the healing process is promoted by the body being exposed to very cold temperatures – is proven to repair muscles and reduce pain in runners and athletes.

- From a self-esteem perspective, winter weather can give us a body-image boost. Any pressure you may feel to be bikini-ready evaporates as you focus on what your body really needs: warmth and comfort. This break from self-consciousness boosts your mood and confidence and allows you to focus on a positive fitness regime, focused on overall well-being rather than your appearance.

- You get to challenge your mind and body with pastimes only possible at this time of the year: sledging, skiing, curling, snowboarding, cross-country skiing, snowshoe-ing and ice fishing – adventurous pursuits that will get you engaging in the great outdoors in great new ways. Exercising is less taxing on the body in cold temperatures than when it is hot, and, according to *Medicine & Science in Sports and Exercise*, we're actually better and faster athletes in cold weather.

- This might sound a bit topsy-turvy, but you're less likely to get sick if you venture out into the cold. Your body becomes more resilient, the cells that fight infection in the body increasing with exposure to cold.

- You get a youthful glow by just stepping outside. No need for blusher this season, when cold weather has got your blood vessels working extra hard to give you that fresh, rosy-cheeked look.
- Vegetable patches and farms are full of the much-maligned Brussels sprouts at this time of year. They're never as bad as you remember, so get munching to ingest the super-powers of this cruciferous veg (other winter wonders – kale, cabbage and broccoli – are from the same family), which includes decreasing cancer risk. A 225g portion of Brussels sprouts serves up 125 per cent of the daily recommended allowance of vitamin C and 243 per cent of daily recommended vitamin K.

- Cold weather burns brown fat faster than warm weather, so when you feel chilled to the bone, there is a reason for it: your bones may be nearer the surface after a winter freeze. Cold weather also burns calories faster than warm weather, which is good to know as you head into the season of Baileys on ice and Ferrero Rocher pyramids.

- The hazy, fiery winter sun might not be as bright and hot as it is during the other three seasons of the year, but its rays still give us a much-needed dose of vitamin D, which in turn helps to fight off SAD, depression and insomnia.

- Lastly, if nothing else, being out and about during the cold winter months will make you really appreciate spring all the more – and you know how good feeling thankful is for you!

Nice ice

This is the perfect time to push yourself, literally, by pushing yourself off from the edge of an ice rink. Is it a sport? Yes, but more than that it's a chance to be brave and let go of inhibitions and fears, to stop being clingy. Every year we get older, as adult life takes over, things become scarier, but fear can put a harness on our ability to have fun. Ice skating is a symbolically simple way to test ourselves. When I first attempted it, after two ▶

decades of not getting my skates on, I was Bambi on ice, and did a few bandy-legged circuits clinging on to the side, a rambling, fumbling mess of 'Excuse me, I'm sorry', being looped by precocious three-year-olds. But that got boring eventually and I thought: *What is the worst that can happen? A bruised bottom and ego.* I let go. The rush was exhilarating. I held hands with two girlfriends and we squealed with glee. I'd done it.

Reindeer games

Snow and ice offers a million opportunities for outdoor fun, for young and old. Have a snowman-building race: the first one to place the hat on a finished Mr Frosty wins. Blow bubbles on a cold day: they will be harder to pop and take on a bewitching iridescence. If it snows, go outside with some plain black paper and a magnifying glass, and look at the individual flakes and their unique patterns as they fall. Use pine cones and twigs to play noughts and crosses on a bed of snow. Fill spray bottles with a mixture of environment-friendly food colouring and water, and get your graffiti on after a fresh snowfall. Experiment with ice – freeze pine needles, winter berries or small toys into ice balls, then dangle them outside and observe how long it takes them to thaw.

Winter playlist

Get moving and grooving to these ten heart-hugging, party-popping tunes, perfect for this season of home, hearth – and staying warm:

- 'A Hazy Shade of Winter' by The Bangles
- 'Urge for Going' by Joni Mitchell
- 'I Felt the Chill Before the Winter Came' by Elvis Costello
- 'Winter' by The Rolling Stones

- 'A Long December' by Counting Crows
- 'Tenth Avenue Freeze-Out' by Bruce Springsteen
- 'California Dreaming' by The Mamas and the Papas
- 'It May Be Winter Outside (But in My Heart it's Spring)' by Love Unlimited
- 'Merry Christmas Everyone' by Shakin' Stevens
- 'New Year' by Sugababes

Frosty fashion

A tip for getting to enjoy the outdoors during winter is to dress appropriately. This might sound like common sense but, unfortunately, I know from experience that a blue sky can be misleading, and Jack Frost really can nip your toes. The key to staying healthy and snug while braving the elements during the colder months is layering and lovely fabrics. Use many thin, warm layers rather than one or two claustrophobic heavy numbers. That way you can peel off to the right degree when you hit different degrees.

That sweaty ball of steam you become when you enter a building in winter will be less overwhelming if you can strip off efficiently. If nothing else, invest in strong, watertight boots. And pair them with woollen or fleece socks that aren't too tight as to shut the circulation off. If you can, buy a good winter coat. Don't go for fashion, go for timeless function, so you won't have to shell out again for a few years.

It's a myth that most of your body heat escapes through the head, but it's still a good idea to wear a hat to stop your ears freezing off. Gloves are a must – keep a few pairs all over the place (car, handbag, office desk) so that you're never without, and if you're embarking on an epic outdoor adventure, consider hand warmers.

Baby, it's cold outside – so how do you bring nature inside?

Keep up your sylvan connections and nature-loving ways even when you're inside this winter, with these simple tricks:

- **Nature-themed colouring books** are a relaxing way to stay connected to flora and fauna while staying warm and chilling-out indoors. Or, if you're feeling creative and want to freestyle, pull out your favourite photos of treasured nature spots and have a go at painting or sketching them. Any kind of artistic expression like this soothes the mind.

- **Your windows can be your canvas** When the weather is just too freezing to get out, or the slush is making you immobile, prop up a place in the window and look for something you love. Cloud-watching allows you to drift off into a dream, and watching a blizzard come in and settle over your street is nothing short of enchanting.

- **Bring the outside in** via your postman. No, I'm not suggesting anything untoward! I mean the festive season is a great time for mail – fewer bills, more cards from loved ones and little-seen friends – so spend the time indoors really relishing this charming communication with the outdoor world, and pay it forward. Forget e-cards or emails; choose cards that lift your spirits – reindeers, log fires and snowflakes, Mother Nature is the perfect muse – and send them sealed with a loving kiss and a heartfelt message.

- **Go to a Christmas tree farm** and drag a fir tree home. Plastic just isn't the same. Then spend time decorating it with collected ornaments and trinkets from bygone years. You can also add items from the natural world: paint and glitter fir cones and acorns. Use mistletoe and ivy to make wreathes and mantelpiece decorations. Fruit also makes for pretty decorations – a kumquat and red-ribbon wreath anyone? A sprig of holly in a glass vase is a simple yet stunning addition to a coffee table.
- **Build the perfect log fire**, if you can. Go out into the woods to forage for suitable sticks and small logs.
- **Create a mini nature scene** in a glass bowl, with fake snow, bird ornaments and real pine cones and leaves. For a splash of colour, add the deep redness of pomegranates or that stocking favourite: a tangerine. Or fill glass bowls with cranberries and balance lit tea lights on top of them for a ruby glow.
- **A collection of pint-sized pine trees** make a foresty feel-good display on a dining-room table. Spray with red and gold glitter or snow-in-a-can for a whimsical look, or leave them bare in their natural state. The scent is wonderful and they look Lilliputian-lovely.

O Christmas tree, O Christmas tree, how lovely are thy branches

The festive season is a pretty exciting time for forest-therapy lovers – am I right? Because we get to bring a big, beautiful, fragrant, vibrant tree into our home! We get to look at it all day and all night if we want to. We get to take pictures of it, of the cat next to it, of the children decorating it. We get to sniff it. Yes, an artificial one might be symmetrical, reusable and not as messy but, merry Christmas to you – a TREE! A real tree in your house! And anyway, real trees are the best choice for Mother Earth. Fake ones are made of materials such as polyvinyl chloride (PVC) and metal, and cannot be recycled, so they get chucked into landfills when they're out of favour. Real trees are harvested over a number of years, emitting oxygen and providing a habitat for wildlife, often in locations such as under power lines or on steep slopes where other crops wouldn't grow very well. When the sad day arrives when you take your tree down (traditionally on the day after the Twelve Days of Christmas, January 7), your tree can take on another natural life as recycled mulch, compost or be moved to your back garden as a shelter for birds. Maintain the spirit of the season by hanging birdfeeders from it if the tired branches will take it.

Can hibernation heal?

In this socially busy season of non-stop partying, you may want to spend some time on your own, and make like a forest creature and hibernate for a while. If you're going to hide away, make it worth it: treat yourself to thermal pyjamas and toasty socks, ask for new books as Christmas presents, take a break from shaving your legs, bake shortbread, drink hot cocoa and catch up on sleep. Make a corner of your home a refuge, a den, a hideout perfect for hibernating with blankets and cinnamon-scented candles. Because sometimes there are brief moments when we do need to squirrel away from society and do a dormouse.

When you're stuck indoors, you have more time for the deep-and-meaningfuls with loved ones. It's okay if, for a while, in winter you venture outdoors only briefly, to head to a friend's house for a chat or a board-game marathon, or if the dark evenings give you time to prioritise longer phone calls, Skype sessions or FaceTime catch-ups, because there is a therapeutic benefit to staying in touch this way, too. As the world falls into a sleepy state, you can unplug too. This will help you reboot your circuits for the new year ahead. Unwind, disconnect, stop worrying about work emails. Reconnect with yourself and the people you love rather than worrying about staying connected to cyberspace.

Hibernating on particularly icy days also gives you the chance to complete the niggling projects of the year, the things you've wanted to finish for months but have placed on the back burner. Finishing them before a new, fresh year begins will give you a deeply rewarding feeling of satisfaction and achievement. You can read the pile of books that has built up on your bedside table, save all your photos properly, or update your address book, which is useful for Christmas-card sending.

Winter reads

Here are five books to get you mesmerised during a winter's day curled up next to a log fire:

- *Breakfast at Tiffany's* by Truman Capote
- *Little Women* by Louisa May Alcott
- *The Thorn Birds* by Colleen McCullough
- *A Christmas Carol* by Charles Dickens
- *Bridget Jones's Diary* by Helen Fielding

Don't hide away for too long, though. An absence of natural light and the constant presence of electric lighting can throw off your internal rhythms. And, as you know by now, being out on the green scene is like having a therapist who improves every aspect of your life, and throws in lashings of vitamin D and fresh air for good luck. There's also the social impact. Hiding away can become addictive. Saying no to friends, family and fun gets too easy after a while. But you are not a furry forest creature – you have enough food to survive the winter. So be a Santa to your soul and take the time you need to recoup from the year, then answer the phone, accept the invitation, pull on your waterproof boots and get out into the beautiful, sparkling, chilly world with your loved ones and toast it! It will be the greatest gift you could ever give yourself.

Excella, 41

'As much as I love to lie around the beach getting a tan, or rather, I used to be able to do this before I had kids, there is something about the British seaside in the winter. The town itself may be dull, grey and a little bit sad, but to just sit there on the shore, bundled up against the freezing cold watching the sheer majesty and ferociousness of the sea is oddly comforting. I can sit for hours (as long as I have a hot chocolate to keep my hands warm!), just watching the waves and the horizon.'

Winter flowers, greenery and berries

These blooms, leaves and berries are abundant at this time of year and symbolic of the season, so treat your home – and yourself – to a posy if you can this winter:

- Amaryllis
- Camellia
- Holly
- Hyacinth
- Ivy
- Mistletoe
- Pine and pine cones
- Snowberries
- Snowdrops
- Winter-flowering iris

New Year's Resolutions

I prefer setting myself targets in spring, when I seem to shake off the cold and get a new lease of life, or in autumn, when the back-to-school vibe makes me sit down and study what I am doing with my life and how I can improve it. But if you are a traditionalist, there is only one time to look back with self-awareness, and then look forward to a better you – and that is 1 January. For many of us, New Year's resolutions are key to setting an agenda for our health and mental well-being that we can keep over the following 12 months.

Why? Because there is no neater, clearer date to have a fresh start than on the first day of a crisp new calendar, when the overindulgences have been so much that you actually yearn for a time of simple food, no booze and some exercise. You want to take the high jinks down a notch or two and find some peace in nature.

New Year's Day is the perfectly positioned precipice to look back on what you didn't like about last year, to think about what made you feel bad and what made you feel good, then jump off into refreshingly clean ideas and notions. And it feels like the world is willing you on. There is a mass push to take control and improve one's health and well-being on this day, and the positive encouragement is invaluable. We're all in this together, the world is singing to you.

New year, new you – it sounds simple, right? But don't be too harsh on yourself if 'Auld Lang Syne' is still ringing in your ears when you mess one of your resolutions up. It doesn't matter. They are a self-contract, an agreement with yourself.

Plan a reset date. The first of February is just as good as 1 January in my book. The worst thing you can do is feel disheartened and throw away all your life-enhancing dreams, ideals and plans because you feel beaten. And don't be too self-critical if you're not noticing changes fast enough. Any good change is worth doing, however insignificant it might feel at first. Good luck!

Catherine, 34

'One cold, winter's day when my daughters were toddlers, we needed to get out of the house. We braved a deserted park, wrapped up against the dropping temperatures in appropriate weatherproof gear, the girls' moods improving with every gulp of brisk air. That was until they got stuck in a patch of gloopy mud, fell over in it, and ended up getting covered from head to toe. I had to strip my two squidgy girls down to their nappies, then gave one my jumper and the other my coat, before racing home. What could be considered a nightmare is now one of my favourite memories.'

MINDFULNESS MINUTE

Sit out in nature if you can, or find a quiet, calm place indoors. Close your eyes and concentrate on your breathing. After a few deep, careful breaths, think of a Christmas tree – the one you have up now, or the perfect one you saw in your local pub's window, or the one your parents used to have in your childhood home. Allow your mind to be dazzled by the tinsel and fairy lights. Imagine you are inspecting the tree closely – the pine needles, your reflection in the baubles, the ornaments that warm your heart. Allow the excitement and sparkle of the season to wash over your entire body and fizz into your brain. In your mind's eye, you begin to glitter and glow with life and joy. This is how your loved ones see you. You are this beautiful. This is why those who love you smile when they see you or hear from you. Remember that.

7

Parenting in Plein Air

'Let nature be your teacher.
She has a world of ready wealth,
our minds and hearts to bless –
Spontaneous wisdom breathed by health,
truth breathed by cheerfulness.'

William Wordsworth

I could never have imagined, six years ago, before I was a mother, how crucial the philosophy of parenting in plein air was going to be to me. Yet very quickly, as my son's toddlerdom began, I realised that the current 'indoor childhood' way of doing things would be toxic to me as much as to my son, William. Adding my daughter, Matilda, to the mix two years after my son's birth furthered this belief. Inside our house, every tantrum was amplified, every mood shift heightened, every stern word harsher – and the feeling of entrapment that so many mothers (and fathers) feel when suddenly thrust into the 24/7 life of caring for little people, was suffocating. Family life within four walls can feel claustrophobic. So, if this is you, you know what I'm going to tell you to do, right? Yup. You need to al fresco your family ASAP.

Mother Nature, the nurturer

Desperate to become a mother for two years, and suffering two miscarriages before William came along, I was shocked at the negative mental effect becoming a parent had on me. The tiredness was expected, but the feelings of hopelessness combined with an overwhelming sense that I'd somehow lost my identity really took me by surprise. I wasn't suffering from post-natal depression, I was one of the lucky ones, but I was exhausted, sore and irritable.

Good news: nature can help with baby blues

Take care of your body and brain: take a long walk with baby in a pram; avoid alcohol and choose refreshing teas; sleep when the baby is sleeping; pick up healthy food at the supermarket; get dressed and washed every day (no living in your PJs); and be kind to yourself. Walk to the nearest shop for a newspaper every morning, meet friends for a walk around the park rather than in a café, or even take baby round your garden and tell it the names of the flowers and insects. Marvel in what your body has just done and don't get caught up with dishes, housework or losing weight. Enjoy your moment, mama.

Advice from mama bear . . .

. . . and an outdoorsy *kvinne* (woman) from Norway:

'If you don't do anything else, just do this one thing, please for me,' my very sensible, kind-hearted mother said to me soon after William's birth. 'Treat yourself to a shower or bath every day and get outside. Walk! Take in some sights, some scents, and some fresh air. Get out of the house!' We were living in Louisville, Kentucky at the time, a state famous for its meandering, hilly horse farms and fields filled with smoky-scented tobacco sheds. Spurred on by my mum's advice, I got up and out, like a grizzly bear, shaking off months of sleeping in a dark cave, and started to remember that there was life beyond sore boobs, scary nappies and bouts of weeping.

My morning constitutional – a slow push of the pram under a canopy of magnolia blossom to the grounds of a quaint antebellum mansion and back – brought me back to life. To feel the sun on my face and a breeze at my back was restorative. And William's cries didn't rattle my nerves so much when matched by birdsong.

At this time, I was also lucky enough to be befriended by Solveig, a Norwegian in Kentucky (yes, that happens), who joined me for daily nature experiences, filling me in on her nation's philosophy of living in fresh air, persuading me that we could get our coffees to go and march up and down our tree-lined high street instead of sitting on our bottoms. As we walked, she told me that Norwegian child-rearing involved giving offspring every chance to find their own feet and freedom outdoors, in all four seasons, free of over-regulated agendas and helicopter parenting.

Safety, of course, came first, but *friluftsliv* parenting meant allowing your children to get dirty, get a bit chilly, and do things that slightly scare you and the child, such as climbing a tree and picking up bugs. The American philosophy I was exposed to was very much about momma and baby hiding inside for the first six weeks, and continuing that overly protective way of parenting, pushing academics and schedules over fun and freedom, fearful of germs or judgement. I was so lucky to have a sensible English mum and a Norwegian '*friluftsliver*' to help me decide what kind of mother I wanted to be from the very beginning.

By the time my second child, Matilda, arrived, I was living in Los Angeles and was a certified life coach. I remember working with a young mum who was struggling with a husband who spent all his time in the office and two young children who didn't sleep. I swear that what helped her as much – or more, I hate to admit – as my relationship with her as a sounding board and champion was the fact that I insisted our sessions took place while we walked, pushing the children, along the beach. Yes, I had a programme for her to follow, and ideas and advice to offer about handling her circumstances, but I can honestly say that I don't believe my training was a patch on the restorative power of the Pacific Ocean.

Child's play

Reconnecting with nature was a tonic for me as a new parent, and we shouldn't underestimate the impact it can have on the youngest, sweetest souls either. The magic of seeing a two-year-old have a conversation with an earwig is not to be underestimated. We can reverse the current trend for the fake and superficial, the immediate and the plastic. We have the power, fellow parents, godparents, grandparents, school teachers! We can get our kids outside, connected to the earth and loving nature again. We can encourage them to embrace freedom, fresh air and dirt. And remember: we need to lead by example. The more we *show* the children we care about how keeping fit and being outdoors is fun – rather than telling them – the more they will believe us.

How to: create a scavenger hunt for your kids

First choose a theme, determined by the season and the location. List items that require kids to use multiple senses: to look, to feel, to smell. Give a mix of easy-to-find and more challenging items, depending on the ages of the children. Don't overwhelm them – keep the list to under ten things, and don't forget to give them a pen and paper to make notes. Set a time limit, and they're off! Tell them not to remove anything, just spot it and tick if off their list. Have a winner if you want to, but perhaps the whole family could be rewarded for discovering things together – sharing a delicious snack as a prize.   ▶

Why don't you revisit your own childhood – and the previous generations' – for inspiration? Building secret dens away from annoying parents' eyes, kicking the curb planning your future until dusk, or plucking berries and preparing a feast for imaginary friends. These things made me – and my mother, and my grandmother. They made my buddies. I gained so many memories doing this stuff. I can still hear the burbling trickle of the local stream. I can still smell the scent of my rose-petal-coated fingertips as I drift off to sleep on summer evenings. Nature was my ally, the backdrop to my adventures.

Today, as a 41-year-old, I still treasure the forest path behind my parents' house and take it every time I visit them, remembering the exact spot Andrea and I got ambushed by a random cow, where James and I played James Bond, or where I nearly wet myself laughing when a caterpillar fell off an oak tree and landed on a petrified Donna's head. It would break my heart if, reminiscing on their youth in the golden years of tomorrow, all my children would feel nostalgic for was the cold metal of an iPad or the smell of furniture polish. In fact, the only part of nature I don't want them to experience is head lice. We did that once, all three of us plagued by those resilient little bugs for days, and I don't think I'll ever feel itch-free again. But, nits aside, there is no part of nature I don't want my children to explore or be enveloped in.

This concept of 'indoor childhood' that is generally accepted as standard these days has to be stopped. What is it? It is the term given to a sad fact of modern life: that childhood is less and less spent outdoors. Too many – the majority – of children in the UK and US are no longer being immersed in the creative, explorative world of their natural environment, a place where social skills are polished, and energy and emotions released in a healthy way. Today, statistics show, children are inside playing alone or enduring a very structured indoor post-school routine that allows little, or in worst-case scenarios, no free play. Your mini-me may be able to play the violin and speak Mandarin, but he could be miserable. Young children need to move.

Let me check my schedule

When I was a kid, my neighbours and I would simply knock on a friend's front door and ask if they wanted to come out and play. Now, we live in the over-organised and constructed world of play dates. Fun needs to be booked weeks in advance. There's a lack of spontaneity and adapt-ability, and designated worthy (and often very expensive) pursuits are put first. And kids are frustrated. I noticed recently how my daughter was dragging to ballet class – something she once loved had become a chore. 'I just want to play with baby Kate next door!' she said forlornly, as after an already action-packed day of Montessori school, I wriggled her into a leotard and drove her 20 minutes to class. I had to think: was the ballet obsession hers or mine?

As a mother, getting outdoors into the fresh air and slowing down in nature has become an even hardier, perennial part of my life than ever before. In fact, it's become more than a practice, it's become a central core of my parenting philosophy. A recent survey by Persil of 1,200 parents of 5- to 12-year-olds from ten countries, found that British children were among the most housebound in the world, spending twice as much time on screens inside as they do playing outside. And according to a report by the Alliance for Childhood, American children of today spend 50 per cent less time in unstructured activities than children did in the 1970s. Parents dictate their schedules, and this barrage of classes and activities (often chosen around a busy parent's schedule rather than the child's interest) mostly take place inside. Increasingly, even young children have little unstructured play time and little outdoor time, neither of which, the Alliance for Childhood believes, foster creativity or happiness.

By allowing this fashion for indoor childhood to continue, we parents are making a rod for our own backs. We're letting a tiger mum obsession with learning and winning get in the way of what our child really needs. I remember at my son's first day of school meeting other parents who were asking about reading levels and maths tests. I asked how long lunch and playtime was. 'My son is like a dog. He needs to be let out for walks and play regularly,' I joked, from a miniature chair, knees up round my earlobes. My question was greeted with a mixture of shock and disdain, but afterwards, a few mothers came up to me and said 'That's my boy too! He needs freedom and exercise.' Admitting this shouldn't be a dirty secret. It's obvious, surely! But in these competitive days of academic exams, our children are missing out on the basics. We're so scared about societal expectations and safety that we're clipping our baby birds' wings before they've even learnt to fly. We need to let them soar, people, soar! We don't want trophy children, like trophy wives but in miniature: mute creatures who look perfect but are miserable. We want real-life thinking, funny, dirty, brave, quirky, streetwise children, who get to develop their interests and talents at their own rate. This will fill them with a passion that they will be able to maintain throughout their life, rather than drain them before they've even really begun.

Being media savvy

Screen time has its place – I'd never get a bath or be able to make dinner if I didn't allow my two time with Peppa Pig or Minecraft – but balance and restrictions are key. In a recent study, the American Association of Pediatrics (AAP) recommended that parents prioritise creative, unplugged playtime for infants and toddlers. For school-aged children and adolescents, the idea is to balance media use with other healthy behaviours. The study found that problems happen if media use displaces physical activity, hands-on exploration and face-to-face social interaction in the real world, which is critical to learning. Too much screen time can also harm the amount and quality of sleep. The AAP suggests that two- to five-year-olds are restricted to one hour of media per day, while six-year-olds and older can have longer if it does not interfere with adequate sleep, physical activity and other behaviours essential to health. Bedrooms should be media-free for all ages.

How do you ignore the moaning?

Children moan and whine a lot. It's one of their less attractive qualities. They also throw tantrums, which is even worse, because they're embarrassing too. I don't know whether it's because they are tired and feeling lazy, or because they have a shocking Topsy and Tim addiction fed by the television screen, but sometimes my children refuse to budge outside, cementing their bottoms to the sofa. Trying to get them out into sunlight is sometimes painful. You know what I mean, right? If you don't want to go the earplug route, I suggest bribing them with fun outdoor gadgets like a compass or binoculars, feeding their sugar cravings with the promise of 'smores' – a toasted marshmallow and chocolate sandwich which is the perfect outdoor eating treat – after play time or, quite simply, tickling them out the door. Yes, a visit from the Tickle Monster never fails to get a child (a) moving; and (b) smiling. He even works on teens.

If all this fails and they're still grumbling at you trying to do your best and be a good parent, blast them with Joni Mitchell's 'Big Yellow Taxi' until they run for the hills. As soon as they're out and about, they'll forget what they were ever moaning about. I promise.

Nature reads

Ten books for under-eights that inspire a child's love of nature:

- *The Complete Brambly Hedge* by Jill Barklem
- *The Other Way to Listen* by Byrd Baylor and Peter Parnall
- *Children of the Forest* by Elsa Beskow
- *The Enchanted Wood* by Enid Blyton
- *The Tiny Seed* by Eric Carle
- *Maisy Grows a Garden* by Lucy Cousins
- *The Wind in the Willows* by Kenneth Grahame
- *Tidy* by Emily Gravett
- *We're Going on a Bear Hunt* by Michael Rosen and Helen Oxenbury
- *A Little Guide to Trees* by Charlotte Voake

Is it a bird? Is it a plane?

No, it's Green Man – the superhero we've been searching for!

There are numerous studies telling parents why indoor play is detrimental to children's growth, and in some forward-thinking communities, forest kindergartens are a popular choice. In Germany, where the concept began, they are called *Waldkitas*, and young children are taken out of the classroom and into forest environments. Studies have shown that graduates from such schools have a clear advantage in cognitive, creative and physical ability.

Encouraged to be free on the green scene, children learn on multiple levels with each new experience. With all the imaginary castles, lands, creatures and friends, the brain develops at a much faster rate than for those who play indoors. They have to rely on fantasy and make-believe, recall stories of knights and dragons and folk of the faraway trees. There are many positive effects seen in kids given a fresh-air life to live. Not only do they become better learners and do well in school, but they are also more fun to be around (and so they make more friends) – everyone wants to play with the kid with the active imagination! Consequently, children will be much happier because, hey, they're smart and they have a lot of friends. All of this is from just playing outside.

How to: make a daisy crown

Pick some daisies with fairly long stems. Teach your child to use their thumbnail to cut a 1cm slit into the stem of a daisy. Once you have created a slit, take another daisy from your collection and pull the stem through the slit of the original daisy. This creates the chain-like effect. Repeat this step as many times as you please to achieve the desired length for the daisy crown. Connect the first daisy to the last daisy, making an inch long slit in the last daisy on the chain so that you can pull the whole flower through. Then crown a friend!

A study of 18,500 people conducted by the University of Derby and the Wildlife Trust showed that there was a scientifically significant increase in people's health and happiness when a connection to nature and active nature behaviours (such as feeding the birds and planting flowers for bees) was sustained over a period of months. The research showed that children exposed to the natural world showed increases in self-esteem. It explained how these interactions had taught children to take risks, it had unleashed their creativity and given them a chance to exercise, play and discover. In some cases, nature can significantly improve the symptoms of ADHD, providing a calming influence and helping with concentration.

Walking and singing

Ten songs for under-eights to sing while taking a nature walk:

- 'Rain, Rain, Go Away'
- 'Incy Wincy Spider'
- 'Round and Round the Garden'
- 'Teddy Bears' Picnic'
- 'Mulberry Bush'
- 'Mary, Mary, Quite Contrary'
- 'Lavender's Blue'
- 'I Love the Mountains'
- 'I Had a Little Nut Tree'
- 'Rabbits'

Not only are there emotional and psychological advantages to playing outside but there are also even more physical advantages. Obviously, if a child is playing outside he or she will be way more physically fit than the child that stays indoors, sitting watching television or an iPad. The great thing about this is that it can have long-lasting effects, as proven by a study by an Australian team of nutritionists and academics in the *International Journal of Obesity*. Years down the road, the child will still be more active and less likely to be overweight. If you think about this, it makes perfect sense: teach a child when they're young to love moving around outdoors and they will love it – and move – for ever.

Nervous for the future but prompted by studies like this, the NHS has released new guidelines regarding children and activity, suggesting kids aged between 5 and 18 should get at least one hour of activity outside every day, giving a stern warning to parents that the sedentary, indoor lifestyle children are currently living can lead to serious problems later in life, such as heart disease and type-2 diabetes.

In her book *Toxic Childhood*, ex-head teacher Sue Palmer argues that being active outdoors allows children to build emotional resilience, and I've seen this with my own children, now six and four years old, as they race around the quarry and woodland next to their school every afternoon, picking themselves up after scrapes and falls or tussles with friends, and negotiating their way through arguments over stick and twig possession. Away from strict structure and adult-guided time, they can explore who they are and how they work with others. Palmer has seen over the years in her work in schools (as I am seeing right now as a mother) that playing outdoors increases a child's adaptability and social skills. Climbing trees, making dens, playing football and making new pals at a park teach confidence and resilience – a gutsiness we need to promote in the next generation.

Eliza, 3

'Flowers are really beautiful. I love them, so I hug them and kiss them. Purple ones are my favourite and I like them when they smell like dirt. I pick them to give them to Josie and Adrienne and everyone who is my best friend. Everyone in the world is my best friend, actually.'

Now here's what the experts say about the disadvantages of indoor play; the worst news first. Researchers have grabbed on to the concept of Louv's nature-deficit disorder, discussed in Chapter 1, and how it changes children. Basically, this means that they know that not playing outdoors and within nature (such as walking, foraging, hiking or camping) is really detrimental for kids. Environmental psychologists Nancy M. Wells and Gary W. Evans have even gone so far as to study whether the closeness between where families live and nature affects their children. They have collected data from 337 children aged between 9 and 12 to see how interacting with the outdoors acted as a buffer to stress that could impact their self-worth and well-being. They found that children who lived closer to nature, and had more opportunities to be in the natural world, were less stressed out with life. They also found that children who had a more natural day-care setting (think: less plastic, more wood, and less concrete, more grass) had better motor coordination and could better concentrate and pay attention.

For children, nature provides an outlet to get away from life's stressors in our fast-paced, technological world. Nature slows us down, lowering blood pressure, as we appreciate its natural beauty. Basically, then, when kids don't play outside in the natural world, they miss the great benefits that nature provides.

My children and their friends play in the forest a short walk from their school most afternoons, year-round, in the rain, with a cold, sometimes with bruised knees, having sword fights with sticks and chasing butterflies – simple things that were so important in my own childhood but that are so easily forgotten when there's the lure of an iPad or television. Even my daughter's most outlandish threenager tantrums can be quietened with a collection of freshly picked flowers, a march along a muddy path or an encounter with a wiggly worm. My washing may pile up with this type of lifestyle, but my sanity has been saved.

Art smart

This chapter isn't just about you making your kids feel and act better by using nature, they can help you out using nature too. Set them art projects either using things from nature or inspired by nature, and use their work to enliven your work area or home. Right now, above my desk, I have an awesome and colourful collection of rainbows and ocean waves that really brighten up my life and remind me of two things that are deeply important to me even when I'm not embracing them: my children and the outdoors.

Becoming an enthusiastic fresh-air family

Don't assume that family reunions have to happen in homes or restaurants. Rope in granny and granddad and spend quality time outdoors. And no, a pub garden does not count, even if you are mindful of the flowers in the hanging baskets. I mean actually engaging with the outdoors and the children you love! Here are some ideas for fun activities:

- **Get an allotment** or join a local gardening club. Reward your child with packets of seeds, then follow the blooms and harvests. Build up a green-fingered community in your neighbourhood with friends of a similar age. Many schools run gardening initiatives after school or at weekends, so get involved, or speak to other parents about setting one up. The kids and parents can work together to grow salad and vegetables for the school canteen or flowers to give to their teachers on their birthdays.

- **Take indoor toys outside** Why do we always assume Lego castles have to be built in bedrooms and living rooms when outside we can dig a moat to surround them? Why should a doll's house stay pristine and clean when outside they are majestically turned into a stately home with grand gardens? And any dirt means having to clean – another fun activity for little hands. Just think how much more realistic your Sylvanian Family animals will look when they're taken out of their plastic box and played with at the foot of a tree!

- **Become an animal detective** With a notebook and pencil, venture outside to search for homes of the cute and wild. Look in trees, up trees, under stones, in rivers and lakes, and in meadows. Nests, hives, burrows, webs and dreys – they all count. Check them out carefully and respectfully – safety first – looking at how each animal has made their home. Admire the hard work and time that went into each construction. If you're lucky, you might find one in the middle of being built, so sit and watch for a while. Make notes and drawings to take home, then research about it more when you get back to your own hard-earned home.

- **Try a game of outdoor opposites** with a friend. Make a movement or strike a pose and get your partner to do the opposite. Jump high, crouch low. Stand completely still, wriggle wildly. Pull a happy face, make a sad face. Take it in turns to test your minds and your bodies.

- **Live a bug's life** Take off your shoes and squelch, even if in your own back garden. Talk about the sensations and the differences between grass and soil. Let creepy crawlies climb up your legs. Impersonate their movements. Discuss what each creature eats and drinks, how they reproduce, who their natural enemies are.

- **Write down your name on a piece of paper**, and get everyone else in your group to do the same. Now, set a time, then go! Find an object in nature that starts with each letter of your name. If the differences are too difficult or large – such as Tom versus Thomasina – perhaps take the challenge but using the same word so no one has an unfair advantage (Petal? Raindrop? Your surname?). The first one to get each letter wins.

- **Go crabbing** Head to a special seaside spot, crustacean causeway or rockin' rockpool. Tear uncooked bacon into small pieces and tie them to a piece of string (or a specially crafted crabbing rod if you're terribly into this idea). Dangle the meat treat into the water until you feel a tug of weight, gently pull the string up and see what you've got. Place the crabs into a bucket filled with the same water that they live in. Look for markings, sizes and injuries, then return them – carefully and slowly – back to their world. Be careful of the kid crabs – their pinchers are the sharpest! And no, you can't keep any as a pet, and no, dad can't cook any for his dinner.

- **Practise your maths** and test your observation skills by counting creatures as you take a walk. Take a pencil and pad and keep a tally chart of all the different species of animals you see – including the neighbourhood cats and dogs. After a good walk, and a good bit of critter counting, sit for a while and work out some statistics. Which animal was most common? Were there more squirrels than bumble bees? What is the most populous creature in your street? How many brown bugs were there? How many black dogs?

- **Make the most of a blustery day** by going outside and old-school with your kid. If you haven't got a kite, make a paper aeroplane. Can't remember how? Take a piece of A4 paper. Fold your paper in half lengthways, making sure the crease is deep, then unfold it. Fold both of the top two corners of the paper down to the middle crease. Now fold the paper in half. Next take the two flat sides and fold them down, back to the centre, until they are evenly folded down to the bottom. You're ready for take-off.

- **Look for the helpers**, heroes and handy things on a walk around your neighbourhood. Point to the things that make your community the safe place that you love (such as the fire station, a recycling bin, a free library, a zebra crossing). Share stories about your interactions with these people and things, and how they help everyone out – including Mother Earth.

- **Get memberships to the National Trust** and/or English Heritage. Although famous for their austere stately homes and damp castles, many of the venues host special outdoor kids' adventure days, full of education, fresh air and history. And remember, frazzled parents, these places normally have great homemade cakes in their quaint tearooms.

- **Join a kid-friendly mindful nature-walking group** They are dotted all over the country. These slower-paced tree-bathing sessions allow plenty of time for studying flora and fauna and to breathe in lots of those powerful phytoncides.

- **Bring shells and rocks** (ones you're allowed to!) home from a holiday and use them to decorate old glasses and Kilner jars. Avoid superglue and cover any surfaces you're working on with old newspaper to avoid accidents. These pots will make lovely gifts or holiday reminders for you. Reminisce as you stick.

- **Make car washing** in summer a family excuse for a water fight. Dress to get soaked. Go barefoot. Blow bubbles. Jump and pop the soapy orbs.

- **Embrace your inner scientist** Gather fallen petals and mix them with water, crushing them in a bowl with a pestle to make perfume. Search for molehills, anthills and rabbit holes, and think about what each creature uses to dig and build. Measure how big the holes are and explain what is going on under the ground. Go on a nest hunt during spring (but don't get up too close to the nest or the bird might abandon the nest), timing how long the adult birds leave home for and what they bring back to their offspring. Play Pooh sticks, by throwing twigs from a bridge and running to the opposite side while counting to see how quickly the current takes them under the bridge to the other side.

- **Go to a park and look for triangles**, circles, squares and ovals among nature and in things we bring to the park such as balls and picnic gear. Point to and name each shape.

- **Try your hand at pressing flowers**, making sure to choose blooms that are not protected. Give your work as gifts to relatives with a message telling them the meaning of the flowers (information is easily found online or in a gardening book).

- **Get in pairs** and choose who will be 'it' for a game of shadow tag. This is the same as playing tag, but instead of being tapped by whoever is 'it', the 'it' person jumps into someone's shadow, and then it's that person's turn to be 'it'. Play at different times of the day to observe how shadows get longer, shorter and disappear over the course of a few hours and with different weather.

- **Even in grim weather**, when dressed correctly, a few minutes outside is vital and helpful to kids. If you know bad weather is coming, get them out for a last-minute run around to burn off some energy before they're trapped inside. If you're super-organised, you can plan ahead, laying out a mini obstacle course around your back garden or communal park for them to race around even when the rain or snow has hit, rewarding them with a hot chocolate on their return.

George, 6

'I love running. It makes me happy. It makes me stronger. I go to a running club one morning a week and my muscles feel really cool afterwards. All stretched. We race through the trees and around a track – me and my friends. We pretend we're flying.'

The bare necessities of life will come to you!

Kids need to get out, as do their parents – because it makes us better parents. Call it Old Mother Nature's recipe for good living – she knows what she's doing, if we would only listen to her. Friends and I take in stunning views from beauty spots instead of sitting inside a coffee shop, I have child-free and fresh air moments with my husband instead of usual date-night dining in a loud, crammed restaurant, and even – when safe – take solo strolls to process my thoughts, dilemmas and to-do lists. All these changes to my lifestyle have benefitted me and my relationship with my children no end. Stress is toned down when faced with a sunset, even if your voice is still hoarse from shouting 'please put your shoes on' over one hundred times that day.

Find your own little nurturing nature routine with your kids. I promise it will help you in the here and now, and in the distant future, when your kids are long gone and grown and you look back on their youth with rose-tinted glasses. 'The days are long but the years are short.' I hear that a lot and normally want to shout at the older person with the wistful expression who is saying it, but I know they're right. Don't let the moments pass in a blur of television time and stressed-out email checking. Find your thing.

This summer, my kids and I developed a love for lavender. We hunted for it, sniffed it, rubbed it between our fingers and declared 'lavender power' as the greatest healer for all things. We breathed together deeply, stopping for a minute, sucking it down, the three of us united. I know – I hope – that for as long as they live, when they see or smell lavender, their brains will be awash with a feeling of love and exploration, and of me, their often too-shouty fishwife of a mother, not on her phone but playing with them!

MINDFULNESS MINUTE

Each member of the group should choose a flower, a feather or leaf, then sit together, forming a circle. For 60 seconds, pass your finds around the circle, thinking of the first thing you notice – the smell, feel or sound it makes. Place your foraged pieces in the centre of the ring and then take it in turns to tell everyone which item was your favourite and why.

8

Being at One with Nature

'Live in each season as it passes; breathe the
air, drink the drink, taste the fruit, and resign
yourself to the influence of the earth.'

Henry David Thoreau

This chapter is all about taking time for self-care, building self-esteem and making the most of alone time – especially alone time in the great outdoors. The modern world doesn't seem to be built for either of those two things. The frenetic pace of FOMO, competitive work practices and the urbanisation of our lives is taking us away from our basic need for silence, peace, contemplation and nature, and it's hurting us. But a commitment to reconnecting with yourself and the world around you will bring many positive changes, very quickly.

I think we're alone now

Being a social butterfly and a party animal is good, but sometimes being alone with your thoughts and ideas – especially when
coupled with the soul-enlivening, mind-expanding bloom of forests, lakes, mountains and oceans – is invaluable. Solitude is not
the same as loneliness. Solitude is not a negative state. Looking
for it does not mean you are depressed, antisocial or sad; it means
you are self-aware enough to know you need a break from the constant claxons of commuting, children's chatter, cyberspace and
that internal voice telling us we're wrong, bad or could do better.
We are overstimulated and overwrought, overstretched and over-
anxious. Alone time, in a location that makes us feel calm and
nurtured, can soothe, replenish and rejuvenate.

The power of one

There are many physical and psychological reasons to make following your own path a priority:

- Being constantly at the whim of others doesn't give the
  brain time to unwind. Being by yourself without constant distractions gives your mind the chance to unravel
  everything and relax.
- Travelling alone, or starting a new hobby *tout seul*, can help
  you to meet more like-minded people in the long run. If
  you try these things in an already established group, you
  are less likely to be open to new people and new friends.

- Taking on a new challenge? Concentration improves without interruptions, and your productivity will go up too.
- When you spend time alone, you get to silence the voices around you and think and decide for yourself who, what and where you want to be. You make time for others; give yourself the same courtesy.
- We all have an introverted side, however much we try to hide it, and alone time will refill our cup of sociability so that we can mix and communicate better over the course of the following day or week.
- The never-ending whirl of chatter and movement prevents you from thinking deeply and creatively. Be still and let the new emotions and ideas flow. Solitude is the perfect state for specific problem solving.
- Hanging out with yourself is less stressful and can be just as fun as hanging with others. You want to explore a city park and you want to do it now, so go! Why wait for others to fit you into their diary, and then let you down at the last minute? Be your own wingman. That way you get to do exactly what you want to do.
- Being alone in nature will allow you to reconnect deeply with the living world around you without feeling the social pressure to make small talk.
- Taking time on your own could actually stop you from feeling lonely. The more time you spend getting to know yourself and what you want, the easier it will be to truly understand who you want around you and why – and that those who don't give you the warm and fuzzies don't deserve any of your time.

Go, go, solo!

The benefits of being alone are numerous, but I'm not suggesting always
shutting yourself indoors away
from the world, stuck in a rut in
central heating and in front of a
television. The benefits come from isolating yourself from society
to clear your head and de-stress, and the benefits are multiplied
when these moments are taken in nature, out in the natural
world rather than hiding away in your human-made one.

Sometimes it feels awkward being out and about alone,
though, and I understand that. Learning to be alone is hard at
first. I used to have to travel a lot on my own for work, and would
find myself friendless and clueless in new cities all the time. At
first, worried about looking like a loser or weird, instead of getting out and exploring, I'd order room service in my hotel room
and only emerge from my bunker when I had a business meeting.
Something clicked when I turned 30. No one was looking at me,
judging my solo status. They were too busy worrying about whatever was in their own head. That was liberating to realise – unless
you rock the boat or draw attention to yourself, no one is focusing
on you. Soon, I was not only exploring cities on my own, dining
in street pavement cafés and observing the world as it drifted by,
but I was actually choosing to go on holiday alone too.

I remember, aged 32, being dumped by a live-in boyfriend and
being so heartbroken that after a few days of sobbing, my face
looked like it had been stung by 1,000 bees. 'Go away,' advised a girl-
friend, 'go somewhere friendly, and walk and think and chill out.'

'Will you come with me?' I begged, feeling a bit vulnerable in my newly single state.

'No, you need a personal epiphany to appreciate he was wrong for you. You can only process that on your own. Me telling you won't resonate deeply enough. You need to be alone to work out your new identity as a single woman.'

I went into the hills for the weekend and climbed over my hurdles. Alone.

We're all losing the capacity to be alone, even taking our phones into the toilet – I hate to admit that I'm guilty of this on occasion – so we can even feel connected while we're on the loo. Two minutes with our own thoughts seems like two minutes too long. But if we can rediscover the richness in self and solitary moments, we are far less likely to feel lonely, even when we're alone, and in modern times, that is crucial. And we're also more likely to get to like ourselves.

Melanie, 45

'Just sitting quietly on a boulder in the middle of the stream changes me. The water acts as an instant meditation. No techniques needed. The water literally washes my thoughts away. Often, as I leave and start to feel the to-do lists, worries and frenetic energy of the world again, I realise the magnificent gift nature just gave me: a quiet mind and a break from all the constant activity. For my health, I've created a life where nature is a part of my daily experience. Whether it's the mountains, the ocean, a forest, a park, or my back garden it's where I go to heal, to exercise, to relax, to recharge, and for fun! For me, nature is my reset button if I'm feeling overwhelmed, confused or just needing to settle my mind. The answer is always the same. In nature, I can see and feel that everything is alive, and if I go with the intention of being receptive I can receive all the messages nature has for me. It's a profound practice in listening.'

Do you have rushing woman's syndrome?

This new term has been invented by nutritional biochemist Dr Libby Weaver to describe the damaging state of being busy, busy, busy that many modern women find themselves in and are unable to escape from, even when they notice the detrimental effects it has on their health. Analysing how this non-stop lifestyle is affecting our nervous systems, she believes that operating in such a permanent state of stress is turning today's women into anxious, moody and forgetful people who can't say no. Worryingly, she has uncovered the impact this 24/7 circus is having on our hormones, making everyday life – and the already disruptive time around menopause – even harder.

Two of the solutions she mentions in her book, *Rushing Woman's Syndrome*, are to savour solitude, which she describes as a powerful way to let your body recharge, and to take gentle forms of exercise, such as yoga or walking. As a peri-menopausal woman, increasingly a victim of cyclical mood swings and anger, who is self-medicating with silent nature walks, I couldn't agree more.

Why take a solitary walk on the wild side?

When we engage with Mother Nature, connecting with her meaningfully, studies show that we are over- whelmed with awe and comforted in a multitude of healthy ways: we feel positive, we feel creatively stimulated and we feel calmed when surrounded by her wild beauty and earthy vibes. It would be a shame if we missed all these life-improving benefits because we were gossiping about a neighbour, or dealing with a tantrum, or staring at our Facebook page.

Sometimes we want to be social in nature, sometimes we ben- efit from going rural and rustic on our own, when the wonders of the world can wash over us without distraction or interrup- tion. So be smart and safe, then reap the many benefits of going stag in the wild:

- **Trusting your instincts is a must** in nature. The choice of which path to take is important. There is no one to ask for advice, so you learn to rely on yourself. Venturing into nature might feel like a risk, so you learn to become braver and better at making the right decision – for you. Spending time alone in nature will increase your self-awareness about just what you, your mind and your body can do.
- **Learning to listen to nature** will make you a better listener in your everyday life. You'll become attuned

to subtleties and softness. You'll start to recognise the sound of your subconscious and not block it out.

- **You'll appreciate your insignificance**, and therefore the insignificance of present worries or past mistakes, when you're walking peacefully beneath a canopy of towering trees, or alongside the untamed sea. The perennial vastness of nature will comfort you: some things are fleeting, like the seasons. Some things you have no power over, as the trees have no power over the changing seasons. Acknowledging this can free you from minute fears or hang-ups.

- **You'll learn to stop blaming others** and to hold yourself accountable – for stepping on an anthill, or slipping off that rock – which will be valuable in all aspects of your life. Sometimes the buck *does* stop with you. Own it, don't moan about it. Be the solution you seek.

- **Being at one with nature** will also make you feel powerful and strong – you are part of something majestic. You can climb that mountain, swim in the waves, swing from a tree and help to protect and shape the flora and fauna around you for the next generation by making the right decisions today.

- **Heading into nature alone** requires courage and determination, and a cheerleader. And because there is only you, you have to learn to become your own biggest fan. Talk to yourself, sing out loud, release a celebratory 'Yeehaw!' when you do something you're proud of. Self-encouragement is a pretty good skill to have in every aspect of your life, even when you've returned from the woods and you're heading back into work and relationships. Actually, make that *especially* when you've returned from the woods and you're heading back into work and relationships. Give me a Y! Give me an O! Give me a U! YOU!

How to make a solo nature walk spectacular

Five easy steps:

1 Look down at your feet for small creatures, not down at your phone screen for status updates. Be mindful of what you are stepping on.
2 Lose the shoes and gain perspective. If it's safe, let your bare feet feel the grass or sand – even crunchy leaves and mud feel nice if you're careful.
3 You're not a bull in a china shop, you are a nature lover in the wild. Be as quiet as you can. This way, you're more likely to be approached by friendly animals, or wilfully ignored and allowed to observe their daily shenanigans.
4 If you can't quieten your mind as quickly or as easily as you'd like to, distract yourself by focusing on your breathing. Counting slow, deep, rhythmic breaths should keep your mind away from niggles until you relax into your solitude.
5 Enjoy it. There are so many worse things you could be doing right now than having quality you time, observing the changing seasons, in a place of beauty, knowingly replenishing your entire being.

You and yoga

The essence of yoga is that it is a personal journey and a non-competitive practice. It is about individual goals and private reflection. What ideas can be lifted from yoga and taken to all aspects of your solo time, whether you're downward dogging or beach strolling?

- Wherever you are, slow down and breathe deeply.
- Stand rooted to the floor, ground yourself to planet Earth, feel the power of being part of this beautiful world.
- Move with intention, don't waste your time and energy on places and people that you don't want or need.
- The soft gaze used during yoga practice could be useful for everyday life, too. Be cognisant of the world around you, but stay focused on your own role in it and how you feel inside.
- You should only be in competition with your better self, or the you from the past or the future. Make your own place in the world; don't constantly look around to see what others are doing.
- In yoga, the instructor constantly reminds us to notice how our body is feeling. Do this in all practices. If you

feel sad, think of the cause and how it can be remedied. If you feel happy, work out why and hold on to it.

- During a yoga class, breaks are encouraged if it gets too much. If your body – or mind – is tired, wherever you are, it is okay to rest, to say no to things. Be as kind to yourself in real life as you would be in a class.
- Going through yoga movements puts you in the moment, in the present. Living in the moment is another way to reduce worrying about things that we have no control over.
- Namaste. I bow to you. Most yoga practices finish with this, an expression of self-acknowledgement, peace and gratitude. Namaste.

Future fabulous

There is no better time to untangle the torments and to ask yourself some serious questions than when you're on your own, in natural beauty, your brain's constant whirring slowing for a while. Evaluate and re-evaluate when you have the time. Harness nature's invigorating strength, free will and constant renewal to improve your own life.

1 Do I like me?
2 Do I respect me?
3 Am I happy?
4 How could I be happier?
5 What do I need to change or do every day to make that happen?

Journaling your journey

There have been times in my life when writing has worked as therapy for me. The best example I can share was when I lost a much-longed-for first pregnancy at 14 weeks. Grief-stricken, I turned to words for solidarity, support and self-expression. When I couldn't articulate my despair to my family, and I sat mute to the concerns of my husband, pen and paper became my only tools of survival. I would sit in our garden and write countless poems, then tear them up, or read them over and over again, pages of my diary falling apart, dampened by tears, covered in scrawl. The self-revelation was powerful; each sentence allowing me to process and clarify my feelings around my loss of identity and motherhood. It didn't have to be good, I didn't have to edit it, I didn't have to share it.

I happened to be taking a literature class at this time on trauma narrative with Dr Suzette A. Henke, a professor I felt comfortable sharing my personal situation with. She informed me that she had coined a term for this journaling process I and countless other people had gone through: scriptotherapy. Dr Henke explained to me how we'd been using words to heal for centuries – in letters to siblings, in diary entries, in declarations to partners that no one would ever read.

Far from being a vain, self-centred approach to healing, as I had feared, scriptotherapy – or journaling – is undergoing something of resurgence, and it's popular within modern psychology thanks to its ability to offer healing without confrontation, to give closure without reproach. Writing can unleash the subconscious even more than Freud's 'talking cure'. Nothing is repressed because we feel we have control over the ink and paper.

Art therapy, like journaling, is another great way of working through your thoughts and emotions. Creativity allows you to intuit, feel and understand yourself and to remove roadblocks to self-improvement. To take a sketchpad or easel to a peaceful spot in the wilderness to draw or paint your pain using the landscape and your imagination, is remedial. Venting on paper – with a pen, pencil or paintbrush – is a safe haven, a private place, where you can truly be yourself and begin to heal with honesty. Where better to heal than in the wilderness, when our temperaments are already improved by the fresh air, phytoncides, vitamin D and beauty – when art and nature mix to mend the broken spirit.

Treva, 38

'I made the decision to end my first marriage five years ago. To escape the prison that had become my house, I went to the woods. Every morning I tossed food into my trail pack and escaped with one goal: to get lost. I rarely saw another human while I was out. From sun-up to sun-down, I rested in the woods. I would spread my blanket on the ground and lie down. Often, I fell asleep for hours, something I couldn't do at home. One day, as I napped reclining against an old poplar tree in a shallow ravine, I was awakened by a buzzing sound. I opened my eyes and found myself face to face with a ruby-throated hummingbird. He must have been attracted to some bright colour near my head, because he just hovered, only an inch from my face, for about a minute. Hummingbirds are amazing creatures. They exert so much energy during the day that their little bodies actually enter a state of torpor at night so that they can recover. I found similar comfort in the woods. I didn't have to be anyone or anything in the woods. The smells and sounds took away all of the anxiety of what to do next. Next simply didn't exist out there.'

Me, myself and meditation

Taking time to meditate isn't a luxury. It will save you time from worry and feeling run down in the long run and it really is as simple as being still, closing your eyes and clearing your mind. Meditation is just a special word for musing, reflecting and contemplation. There are many apps and YouTube videos available to help you get started – and you *should* start. Scientists from the University of California and Harvard Medical School got together to compare the benefits of taking a holiday and doing regular meditation. They used 64 female novice meditators between the ages of 30 and 60, and 30 experienced meditators from the same demographic. The women were sent to the same resort, half taking part in a meditation programme, the other half not. Surveys and blood samples were taken from the women at the start and end of the six days, and after ten months. The women who meditated showed fewer symptoms of depression and anxiety than the ones who hadn't, the blood work showing significant and positive changes related to immune function and stress response.

MINDFULNESS MINUTE

Sit cross-legged in a quiet spot that radiates harmony and regrowth; a peaceful spot off a favourite forest trail would be ideal. Close your eyes and practise taking full, deep, rhythmic breaths. Now imagine that you are connected to the ground you are sitting on. Think of your body as part of the forest, your roots pushing and weaving their way down through the soil, intermingling with other trees and vines. Now imagine being lifted, stretched and pulled towards the sky, your arms dancing in the breeze with the surrounding leaves and branches as they reach for the sky overhead. Keep breathing and take the minute to appreciate how you are linked with this place of beauty, and harness the power you have within you.

9

Couples' Countryside Cure

'The sunlight claps the earth, and the
moonbeams kiss the sea: what are all these
kissings worth, if thou kiss not me?'

Percy Bysshe Shelley

Humankind has always been in love with nature, from worshiping the seasons or the weather as gods and goddesses in ancient times, to honouring Mother Nature today in drumming circles and sculpture gardens. The romantic attachment we feel to the living world has inspired poets, novelists, artists, playwrights, musicians and filmmakers for centuries. The Romantic poets – Byron, Keats, Coleridge, Wordsworth and Shelley – felt the great allure artistically and philosophically of the idea that there is a deep connection between nature and man: that nature is man's teacher, God and everything that matters; and that the urban should not overpower the pastoral. Over two hundred years later, we still agree that Mother Nature is our greatest muse, most loyal ally and sweetest obsession. It is no wonder, then, that interactions between lovers are deepened and enriched when she plays a part in their story. Nature improves human nature.

If you like pina coladas . . .

Making time for each other, free from distractions, is crucial for healthy, sustainable coupledom, and getting back to nature – blowing off the cobwebs from an old, dusty relationship – can give it the boost that is needed. Just think back to that classic love song, 'Escape', when the protagonist, in a tired marriage, places a personal advert in a newspaper looking for a lover to make him happy again. 'If you like pina coladas and getting caught in the rain,' he sings, asking for his true love to write to him. The irony is, of course, that his wife is the woman who responds. She's been desperate to share cocktails, thunderstorms and beach romance too. They'd just lost sight of each other, stopped getting outdoors and enjoying themselves, and they were miserable.

The woodland path of true love never did run smooth. Avoid your love life turning up as a novelty record in the charts by taking steps before it's too late. Embrace each other and embrace the replenishing offerings of nature.

My husband and I had fallen into the trap, until very recently, of thinking that a date night had to mean sitting opposite each other in an expensive, loud restaurant, spending more time talking to the waiter than catching up on our thoughts and worries. We have now changed things for the better, choosing river walks, couples' massages and swimming as our date nights, and they feel so much more intimate and 'us'. Getting out and about outdoors really got us going again.

Get fresh – air that is!

Rolling in haystacks and skinny-dipping – fresh air does something to the libido, no? Outdoor nooky might sound like a good idea when you're in love and feeling sexy, but there are strict rules on public decency, and flouting them could land you in hot water. And I don't mean hot in a good way! So, keep it clean please, keep it clean. And if you can't be clean, be careful.

What can you do to take your love back to nature? Getting caught in a rainstorm and having a drenched snog is obviously the timeless romantic manoeuvre. Obviously! I mean, Andie MacDowell makes puppy-dog eyes at Hugh Grant in *Four Weddings and a Funeral* – 'Is it raining? I hadn't noticed' and boom! Dodgy marriage to rich old Scottish man forgotten, and in the next shot, they're clutching a baby. Having sex on the beach is such a classic they named a cocktail after it, but sand in certain crevices is never nice, and it's too risqué for most, but here are some things you could try:

- **Grab a blanket**, lie down somewhere with a breathtaking expanse of sky, and spend the day chilling out horizontally, cloud watching. Follow the slow drift and look for shapes and patterns. Can you see a rabbit, smoke rings, how many colours?

- **Star gazing** at night from a place with minimal light pollution is magical. Look out for shooting stars. They have left humans in awe since time began, and Ancient Greeks believed that seeing one brought good luck. Carry that luck with you into your relationship.

- **Hire a tandem** bike and explore your local park on wheels. Working as a team deepens bonds and promotes respect.

- **Take on a green-fingered project** together. Rent an allotment, join a gardening club, or take on a challenge in your back garden. The flowers and romance will blossom. Keep seasonal scrapbooks of seed packets, photos and drawings to look back on as the weather and your relationship shifts and re-blooms.

- **Build a log fire**, at home or somewhere permitted outdoors. Cosying up together will put you in Hollywood-romance territory. Rock Hudson and Doris Day eat your heart out. A faux fur rug and cut-glass decanter of brandy are optional props.

- **Whenever you spot a rainbow**, call your partner to tell them to make a wish. Make it a tradition. And the wish could spark some serious flirtation to put a smile on your face.

- **Support each other's climb** to the top – of a mountain, a hill, a topsy-turvy forest trail – then stop at the top to admire the view and celebrate how far you've come. It's always good to bring fresh perspectives to your relationship. Hiking the same path during all four seasons will help you truly witness change and the beauty of passing time and your story's progression.

- **Go on a senses safari** Pick a place – a river walk, a forest trail, a beach path – and explore the scents, sounds, colours and tastes of nature's sensual delights. Feel the leaves or grains of sand, stroke the smooth pebbles in the cove. Such a challenge can be super-sensual and heighten your sensitivity to everything you see and smell, even your partner.

- **Become carefree kids again** Flying a kite, a romantic and colourful pastime that doesn't involve a lot of work but gives ace rewards, is great for windy beach days. Building a forest fort out of branches will build up your communication skills and give you somewhere to snuggle afterwards. Graffiti love messages to one another on your patio with washable chalk.

- **If you need more ready-made laughs**, go to a park, pub or hotel with a super-sized chess set or Jenga in the garden.

- **Set yourselves a seasonal challenge** As each new cycle of life changes, set yourselves a target to achieve within those three months: a glamping trip, a 5k run, a Sunday meditation class – anything that commits you to spending quality time together. At the end of each season look back at the highlights, both individually and as a couple. If something worked really well, make a promise to make it an annual thing, building pleasurable routines and customs into your self-made family.

- **Grab a float or a lilo** and drift off on an ocean wave or lake together. A little adrenalin and the need to cling on tight to someone will reinvigorate your love life, just be sensible and respect the sea.

- **Head to a country brewery** for a tour and tasting, and a chill-out in the beer garden. Play a game of Beer Pong or Fuzzy Duck for laughs.
- **Pick fruit or berries** at a local farm or go blackberry picking. It could be a fun way of telling your sweetheart that you'd still pick them. Grab a punnet-full, then go home and bake together. Yummy.
- **Rent a convertible** and head out into the countryside. Stop for a cream tea or a picnic at a picturesque spot, then drive home for a warm bath as the sun starts to fade.
- **Meet for an impromptu date** after work – when you spot a nice sunset brewing – for a cocktail al fresco at a nearby roof-garden bar. Promise not to look at your phones or talk about work. Live – sup – in the moment.
- **Pitch a tent** in your back garden for a night under the stars – with the toilet and comfortable bed close at hand if needed. Snuggling to keep warm does wonders for rekindling romances. You may need to share a sleeping bag.

Top ten romantic reads

Hire a rowing boat or set up a woodland camp for the day, and drift away in a heaving, heady daze with these novels, my most treasured love stories. Paper has never burst with such passion, I assure you. Surrounded by the birds and the bees – on the page and in the landscape around you – you'll see your own love story in a new light. Reading particularly sensual, moving excerpts aloud to your loved one is positively encouraged.

- *Gone with the Wind* by Margaret Mitchell
- *The English Patient* by Michael Ondaatje
- *Me Before You* by JoJo Moyes
- *Forever* by Judy Blume
- *Pride and Prejudice* by Jane Austen
- *The Fault in Our Stars* by John Green
- *The Notebook* by Nicholas Sparks
- *Wuthering Heights* by Emily Brontë
- *The End of the Affair* by Graham Greene
- *A Room with a View* by E.M. Forster

Animal husbandry

We show off about being the civilised ones, but really we could learn a lot from the natural world when it comes to love, romance and fidelity. Animals don't have as many arguments about who last unloaded the dishwasher either. Some creatures have got this love thang down pat. We call doe-eyed couples lovebirds for a reason: those fluffy birds love to cuddle and are monogamous until their dying day. Other creatures who form lifelong bonds include bats, beavers, foxes and otters. Penguins are monogamous too, but it should be noted that their happy relationship might be possible because they spend most of the year apart. Flamingos get it on in much the same way we do at teenage discos, splitting into a group of boys and a group of girls, then catching each other's eye with some seriously cool dance moves. Seahorses court each other with lots of nose touching and tail holding. Wolves mate for life and take family life seriously, keeping loyally to their pack of male, female and offspring. What animal magic!

Jo, 42

'The romance of nature has never been lost on me. As a ten-year-old, I first learnt to flirt with Boy Scouts on rowing lakes. Then, in my late teens, my first taste of courting occurred during camping trips to the New Forest, tents pitched next to groups of handsome boys, dusky summer evenings filled with possibility. I still can't resist the temptation of spending a few nights with nature every year. Luckily, my husband agrees – and it can be romantic, I promise.'

Making mountains into molehills

Airing arguments in fresh air is always a good idea. Buildings and cities can be pressure cookers for stress, anger and other unhealthy emotions. Slight annoyances take on monumental meaning and we turn molehills into mountains. I feel it. Being stuck within four walls – or on a noisy, polluted street – with someone you're annoyed with makes it worse. I feel trapped, unheard, itchy and frustrated when the world around me won't let my husband and me take a step back, take a breather and take positive action to resolve our issues. I always find that when one of us eventually says, 'Come on, we're going for a walk/to the park/ for a drive along the river', the tension is instantly diffused. The ticking time bomb is gradually dismantled and we either forget about what we were angry about or we can talk about it calmly, distracted not by clutter and clatter but by blue sky or towering trees. You're also less likely to fight before bedtime (which is always a bad idea and often leads to insomnia) if you're taking your issues out into the woods and getting exercise and fresh air.

Once you've found your comfy, calm place in nature to restore peace in your love life, these tips could help you come to a resolution more quickly:

- Don't go straight to blame. Start sentences with 'I' not 'you'. If you get straight into the 'you did this' and 'you are wrong', your partner will go straight to a defensive position.
- Agree that you can take time away from each other if

things get too heated. If you're in nature, you can easily escape to cool off in different directions and then meet up again on neutral territory, whereas if you are in the house, one of you could be trapped.

- Physical exercise releases anger, so if you're feeling frustrated, don't sit – hike your problems out.
- Use everything you've got. The pleasure hormone oxytocin is released by physical touch. Improve the mood by holding hands or looping an arm over a shoulder, even if at first it feels forced. And even if you're not feeling warm and fuzzy, don't resort to harsh tones and formal language. Use affectionate nicknames.
- Follow the advice given in previous chapters about being mindful and present. Don't jump or overreact if you hear something you don't like. Let it sit for a moment, breathe, focus on something beautiful while you think, and then respond. It's like counting to ten but in a more natural, awe-inspiring way.

Sylvan sweet talk and smooth operators

If you need to get it on and don't know how, you might be thinking of throwing some natural imagery out there – roses are bed, violets are blue, or even going down the single-red-rose-wrapped-in-petrol-station-plastic route – but you can do better than that. Keep the natural romance alive with gifts of fresh bouquets of wild garden flowers, air plants, bottles of essential oil misting sprays, membership to a local garden, stately home or park, cactuses in ceramic pots, a subscription to a nature magazine, a beekeeping class, an outdoor wildlife camera, gardening tools and colourful watering cans, a pair of binoculars, a hammock, a starry-sky bedroom light, or an IOU for a forest picnic. If you must do poetry, stick to Wordsworth, the god of pastoral poetics.

Nature's aphrodisiacs

Unfortunately, love potions and magic spells aren't real, but the next best thing is nibbling on an aphrodisiac, many of which you might just have hanging around in your kitchen. For centuries, Aphrodite's natural helpers (she's the goddess of love and sex who gave aphrodisiacs their name) have been said to boost sexual desire with ingestion. How? Nutritionists suggest they have been selected for their ability to decrease stress, increase blood flow or make our neurotransmitters happy: three things that are proven to increase libido. Spice up your sex life by trying some of these herbs and nourishments. Even if you can't feel the physical changes, you could get psychosomatically fruity just knowing you're healthily and naturally eating your way to a tasty time in the bedroom!

- **Almonds** are a biblical symbol of fertility, given out at weddings to this day, and famous for their sweet and sexy scent.
- **Avocados** have been considered a saucy fruit since Aztec times when they were called *Ahuacatl* – which translates as 'testicle tree'.
- **Basil** increases heart rate and blood flow, as does **cardamom**.
- **Celery** contains androsterone and androstenol, two chemicals that give you a glow.
- **Chillies** release endorphins, which make us feel good and frisky. Their heat also gives us swollen lips and flushed skin, two physical signs supposed to show sexual desire.
- **Cinnamon** heats up your body, as does **ginger**.
- **Chocolate** is perhaps the most famous aphrodisiac. It contains phenylethylamine, the same hormone the body releases during sex, which would explain why we all love a Cadbury's Flake so much.
- **Coconut water** increases blood flow and will keep you hydrated during a steamy session.
- **Garlic** (if you both eat it) can work, as it contains allicin, which might increase stamina.
- **Honey** supports testosterone and oestrogen production.

- **Nutmeg** is used in Hindu culture to sweeten the breath to attract a mate.
- **Pine nuts** are loaded with testosterone-boosting zinc.
- **Pomegranates** are rumoured to increase genital sensitivity.
- **Red wine**, unsurprisingly, lowers inhibitions and acts as a relaxer, and it also increases blood flow.
- **Rocket** salad leaves were loved by Romans, who thought that they helped to get a romp going.
- **Truffles** – their scent mimics an opposite-attracting smell similar to pheromones.
- **Vanilla** is a mild nerve stimulant, which might make sexual touch a little more exciting.
- **Watermelon** increases nitric oxide, which opens the blood vessels and speeds up circulation, and the bodily response might be increased arousal.

The eyes have it

Ah, remember in that first flush of romance, when you'd catch your beloved's eye across a crowded room and give a knowing smile? That visual contact was so loaded with passion, intimacy and love back then you'd have to look away. Probably blushing. Or at the very least excited about what would come later, that night and in life. You could literally feel your heart leap when they looked at you. Now, not so much. You're too busy to stare lovingly into each other's eyes anymore. After nine years of marriage and two children, my husband and I were only likely to glare at each other over a wailing toddler's head, a puddle of split milk or a supermarket freezer chest, rather than gaze. We would spend more time looking at our phones than each other. But if the eyes are the window to the soul, we needed to do better, so, we took on a new practice:

Eye gazing This practice of mindfully staring into someone's eyes feels awkward at first, and still weird after a few attempts, I found. It takes you back to the playground and those days of staring competitions and 'whoever blinks first is a loser', but practitioners have found that it helps them to reconnect with their beloved, and it is easy and fitting to do it when you're out in nature, fuelled to focus and think positively by the fresh air and feel-good factors of the outdoors.

How do you give it a go?

1   First, set an intention: what do you want to achieve or reclaim? Intimacy, electricity, comfort? Set the word in both your minds.

2   Next, take a position opposite to each other, sitting or standing, and close your eyes for a few seconds to calm your minds. Breathe in the phytoncides or ocean air. Feel the air. Whoever opens their eyes first can wait quietly for the other one to reach the same space.

3   Gaze into your loved one's eyes. Or eye. Choose the left or the right eye to focus on or you'll feel a bit skew-whiff.

4   You will probably get the giggles when you first begin the practice. Don't worry about it. You might

cry. Don't worry about that. Love is funny and scary.

5   Feel free to blink, too. This isn't a staring contest.

6   Really look. See how your partner's eyes have changed. It's amazing how you can be around someone but never truly look at them. I always find a new wrinkle, a new twinkle, changing colour flecks of light in my husband's eyes. I can tell if he's tired, sad or anxious.

7   Applaud your shared bravery. Eye gazing is bold and bare, with no escape. You are literally face to face. People might dismiss the practice as wimpy hippy-woo-woo stuff, but you need to be strong – or strongly want change in your relationship – to do this.

8   Don't have any expectations other than you'll be spending time in each other's presence without distraction.

9   Even 30 seconds reconnecting meaningfully with someone you love but don't make time for is better than nothing, but aim for 5 minutes or more for a truly mindful rekindling of your relationship.

10 Try to practise regularly, or whenever you feel discombobulated with each other. And aim to keep the connection even during stressful, busy times. Don't turn straight back to your phone screen the minute you've finished.

Solveig, 43

'The unmistakable allure of the Nordic summer shaped my romantic attachment to nature. The summers of my first 25 years were spent on endless hikes through enchanted forests, tiptoeing across mossy floors covered in blueberries, which we picked and then packed in my grandparents' freezer (there were always enough to get them through the next three seasons). I remember threading strawberries, one after the other, on willowy straws, a perfect treat for a day outdoors. This fairytale land of the midnight sun, the fjords, the sea, the mountains we hiked endlessly, drinking from gargling pure mountain streams, was my first love.'

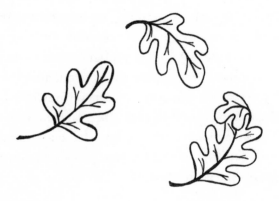

MINDFULNESS MINUTE

Sit back-to-back, holding hands, and close your eyes. Don't talk. Just think. Go back in time to a happy memory: your first date, a wonderful holiday, the birth of a child, a funny moment from that morning. Focus on how you worked together as a team. Think about why you are glad you had that experience with your partner and no one else. Open your eyes and tell each other about your recollection and how it made you feel.

10

Natural Beauty

'Anyone's life truly lived consists of work, sunshine, exercise, soap, plenty of fresh air, and a happy contented spirit.'

Lillie Langtry

There's a reason people spend an abundance of time and money on creams, potions, lotions, make-up and even plastic surgery to get the 'natural look'. Sun-kissed, rosy-cheeked and bright-eyed – these are all physical attributes naturally gained from a life lived outdoors. It's because when you've just taken a brisk walk along the seashore, or a heart-thrilling cycle along a forest trail, you look energetic, alive and young. There is nothing wrong with looking our age, remember, but we do want to look the best we can for the years we have accumulated – God forbid we should be accused of looking decades older. The good news is we don't have to rely on synthetic wrinkle-busters and glow-givers. We can get some forest therapy. To increase the amount of the natural world we get into our diet, healthy practices and lifestyle, means that we must become a true gem, inside and out.

Miss World

Mother Earth offers a pageantry of natural beautifiers if you can only just step away from the harsh lighting in your bathroom mirror – and the self-criticism it promotes – and get out into the world. Forget going under a cosmetic surgeon's knife, try going under a blanket of clouds for a happy, restorative afternoon that makes you feel and look younger. Think about the people who you find delightful to look at, now work out what they have in common: clear skin, a warm smile, a relaxed forehead? They are not attractive because they are a certain weight, age, class or colour, or because they are wearing a certain pair of shoes or because they are dripping in diamonds. No, you find them alluring because they bloom and refresh your eyeballs with their joie de vivre and sunshine glow (and maybe they were genetically blessed too; we can't fight our DNA, of course). Here are some ways they will be using Mother Nature as their beauty guru – and you can too:

- When you're gawping at something beautiful – an ocean, a mountain, a forest – it's hard not to smile. And the good news is that smiling makes you look younger. A study proved that when respondents looked at photos of people with happy faces they guessed their ages as younger than they really were, and much younger than they were in photos of the same person with an angry or neutral expression. Even though smiling creases the corners of the eyes, these are interpreted as laughter lines rather than wrinkles, and smiling uses fewer muscles than frowning so causes fewer wrinkles in the long term too. Going green and grinning will take years off you – and is cheaper than Botox.

- When you're active and actively engaging with nature, you spend less time on your smartphone – which is good news for our posture. Social media addicts are known for stiff necks and stooped shoulders – and the Hunchback of Notre Dame look is so not chic.

- Stress doesn't just mess us up on the inside, but on the outside too. Anxiety aggravates acne, psoriasis and eczema. In the past, during tough times at work or in relationships, I've suffered from a pimply chin and hives on my ankles. Since learning to take self-care more seriously and changing my lifestyle, they've both improved. Take the stress out of your skin by regularly partaking in those mood boosters we've already discussed in previous chapters: long walks, meditation in nature, journaling and marvelling at your surroundings in a favourite natural place. Beauty spots – not spots – for the win.

- Meditation encourages you to soften your gaze and relax your facial muscles, which can ease facial lines caused by tension and make you look more rested.

- Deep sleep is a must for a smoother, youthful look, so regulate your circadian rhythm by getting plenty of fresh air during the day, and tying your body clock loosely into the natural cycles of the sun and moon. It is while you're asleep that your body has the time to restore itself and repair DNA damage from the day before. Set more soothing bedtime rituals (a meditation, a long hot soak, a cup of chamomile tea, a spray of lavender, and a book) than the oft-tempting fiesta of box set, wine and crisps.

- Drinking plenty of water won't clear your skin directly, but it will boost gut health, which in turn helps your skin. It's nature's best hydrator and the obvious choice to fill a flask with on a forest hike or park walk.

- People who feel engaged and connected with the world around them live longer, happier and healthier lives – all things that will make you glow.

How do phytoncides make you handsome?

Forest therapy and phytoncides not only make you healthier, happier, kinder, smarter, more energetic and less stressed – phew! – but, as if that isn't enough, they make you more gloriously gorgeous too. Say what? Spending time in the trees boosts your beauty in multiple ways. It improves your sleeping habits (bye-bye eye bags and dark circles) and it offers up plenty of free, fabulous oxygen – the hottest spa ingredient of the moment. Oxygen is anti-bacterial and anti-inflammatory, and it stimulates the production of collagen, giving that dewy glow we yearn for. Instead of paying a fortune for it in masks, make-up and salon treatments, you can get it free of charge by breathing it in deeply during regular leisurely strolls along a forest trail, away from the toxic air of roads and crowds. Yet, perhaps most importantly, forest therapy and its high dosage of phytoncides beautifies the soul with its awe-inspiring prettiness, removing the greyness of city pollution and the dullness of urban grind from your mind, body, soul – and face.

Nic, 29

'Very often, even during the grey days of a London winter – in fact, especially on these days – I substitute my gym visit for a workout outside in our local park. I love the dose of mood-lifting endorphins, rosy cheeks and the smug feeling afterwards of feeling stoic and hardy! I'm lucky to work near Regents Park in London, and on summer days I like to kick off my shoes and walk and feel the grass between my toes. It reminds me that there's a whole world outside my air-conditioned office, which helps me to put work issues into perspective. There isn't a season when it doesn't improve my mental and physical world to get outdoors. I feel strong and supple, actively and attractively engaged.'

The green scene

Your mum will be happy if you start eating your greens, and so will your beauty regime! Vegetables full of fibre such as broccoli, spinach and lettuce help to clean teeth naturally by preventing plaque from sticking to them. A diet rich in green, leafy veg gives your complexion a kick-start, as the carotenoids (the vitamin-style pigments in fruit and veg) found abundantly in them improves skin tone. Aim for three servings of vegetables a day for a cute complexion.

Fruity face and salad skin

We know that eating natural wholefoods gives us an internal boost, loading us up with vitamins, minerals and antioxidants that in turn will make us all more beautiful inside and out, but what about slathering the contents of our fridge straight onto our face? Can the goodness of ingestible natural foods be recreated when used as a do-it-yourself face mask, hair mask or eye mask? Can coating your wrinkles in coconut make people go nutty for a new, younger-looking you? Can using items from your kitchen save you a bowlful of cash in plumpers and fillers? Yes! And there are even topical treatments to help you through the skin traumas of the harsh weather of winter and the sun-drying season of summer. Let's investigate Mother Nature's pantry – there's lots of cheap, cheerful and quick things in there to make you look as dazzling as the sun.

- **Acai berries** are loaded with antioxidants, amino acids and essential fatty acids.
- **Apple cider vinegar** removes dirt and build-up through its alpha-hydroxy acids.
- Blended **almonds** make an excellent face and body scrub.
- **Avocado** is filled with skin-boosting minerals such as copper, iron and calcium, and yummy vitamins A, B and E, which hydrate dry skin to encourage a fresher complexion.
- **Bananas** provide a good moisture boost and dissipate dead skin cells.
- **Brown rice flour** unclogs pores and softens skin.
- Steamed, mashed then cooled **carrots**, applied as a face mask, stimulate cell renewal.
- It is believed that **cinnamon** can help to plump up the skin and help to treat eczema, thanks to its heavy load of antioxidants.
- **Cocoa powder** is an antioxidant that helps to protect and hydrate the skin.
- **Coconut oil** is antifungal and full of antioxidants, as well as being hyper-hydrating.
- **Coffee grounds** – thanks to the caffeine – work as an exfoliator that boosts blood circulation.
- **Eggs** – whole or just the white – will firm, tighten and moisturise the face.
- **Grapeseed oil** is easily absorbed into the skin for a quick moisture drench.
- **Green tea** – either the ground-up leaves or a brewed cuppa – helps to reduce skin inflammation.

- **Honey** has antibacterial qualities for a healing, clean feeling.
- The freshly squeezed juice of a **lemon** will close pores, mop up oily patches and give your face a shiny brilliance.
- **Oatmeal** is a great gentle exfoliator.
- **Orange** – juice, peel or zest – might help to boost collagen levels for a youthful plumpness.
- Stir up some **sea salt** with **olive oil** for a hardworking body scrub – just don't put it on any cuts (ouch!).
- A potion of finely chopped **parsley** and olive oil balances out skin discolouration.
- The high levels of vitamin C and the protein-eating enzyme bromelain in **pineapple** allow it to work as a collagen-boosting face mask.
- **Pumpkin** masks can reduce the signs of ageing, thanks to this squash's mix of beta-carotene, vitamin A and zinc.
- Packing a punch of vitamin C and naturally occurring hydroxy acid: say hello to skin-brightening **strawberries**.
- **Sugar** in your diet is not good for your looks, but as a body scrub its glycolic acid works wonders.
- **Turmeric**, used lightly because of the bright orange colour, can be applied to skin to ease acne and psoriasis and is rumoured to be a wrinkle-diminisher. The spice is also known for its anti-inflammatory healing properties.
- Slathering organic plain **Greek yoghurt** on your skin helps to repair sun-damaged skin thanks to its lactic acid.

Five quick beauty boosters from your kitchen cabinets

1 Mix two parts water and one part **apple cider vinegar** and apply to your skin with cotton wool to keep pores unclogged and clean. Leave it on for the day.
2 Mix two parts water and one part **fresh lemon juice**, and apply it to your skin with cotton wool to clean and brighten the face. Leave it on for the day.
3 Gently work **60ml olive oil** into your face and leave on overnight as a moisturising mask.
4 Cut two slices of chilled **cucumber** and place over eyes for ten minutes to reduce puffiness.
5 Place a chilled, used **chamomile tea bag** on each eye for ten minutes to tighten and firm the skin.

Natural beauty recipes

Look good enough to eat with these glow-givers from the garden:

Savour the face scrub

Polish and exfoliate away dull skin and the doldrums with this skin-brightening cleanser.

  1 dessertspoon fresh lemon juice
  1 dessertspoon honey
  1 dessertspoon blended oats (see Tip)

Mix the ingredients together in a small bowl, then warm the mixture in the palm of your hand. Smooth onto your face and neck. Leave for five minutes or until dry. Wash off with a flannel or cleansing cloth and warm water, then moisturise as normal or apply a mask.

Tip Get a small batch of blended oats ready for a few face scrubs by putting a handful of porridge oats into a blender beaker and blending them until fine. Store in an airtight container.

Mouthwatering face mask

Plump up and replenish your face with a DIY mask that's good enough to eat:

1 small avocado
1 tablespoon honey
5 strawberries

Mash the ingredients together in a small bowl using a fork. Leave to stand for two minutes. Press evenly onto your face and leave for ten minutes. Wash off with a flannel or muslin cloth and warm water, then moisturise as usual.

Delicious hair mask

Moisten, smooth and gloss your locks by coating the tips of your mane with this mix.

1 tablespoon coconut oil
1 tablespoon olive oil

Blend the oils together in a small bowl, then gently work them into the hair shaft, coating only the dry ends of your hair. Leave for 20 minutes. Follow immediately afterwards with a deep shampoo and condition, then dry and style as usual.

Scrumptious suds

Turn bathtime into a smell-good soak that is doing your mind, body and soul a favour with these natural soothers. Epsom salts are always a solid base, then pour liberal measures of one of the following into your tub, or mix and match them all for a bath full of delectable self-improvement.

- Fresh **ginger**, sliced and placed in the bath, draws out toxins.
- A splash of **milk** has softening and exfoliating properties.
- **Lavender** – the oil or flowers – helps to de-stress the mind and muscles.
- **Oatmeal** soothes irritated or itchy skin.
- **Green tea**, poured in as tea or as a teabag placed in the tub, tones the body.
- **Honey** is moisturising.
- **Coconut** oil softens the skin.
- Pretty, floating **rose** petals are antibacterial and anti-inflammatory.

- **Champagne** or **red wine** can give you a boozy boost when splashed in the bath, thanks to the polyphenols present, which reduce redness and inflammation in the skin.
- **Peppermint** and **eucalyptus** leaves left to float on the water will clear the sinuses.
- A sprig of **rosemary** will clear the mind.
- A couple of **cloves** added to a bath provide stress relief.
- A few drops of **vanilla** are a sweet treat that soothes stress away.

Wakey-wakey! Rise and shine!

Start your morning the right way with an invigorating shower with one of nature's natural wake-up calls: an icy-cold blast, then warm water and a palm full of shower gel containing mint, eucalyptus, watermelon, lemon, lime, lemongrass or grapefruit.

Wear sunscreen

The single most important thing you can do when adopting a life of forest therapy and the great outdoors is to wear sunscreen, because of the risk of skin cancer. This is also the most important thing you can do to slow the takeover of wrinkles, crinkles, age spots and discolouration, which are the visible results of ultraviolet rays on your skin. Even on a cloudy day, the sun is out there – and that's a good thing because you also need some vitamin D. At least 15 minutes three times a week in direct sunlight is recommended to keep your sunshine vitamin topped up. Just get into the habit of wearing a daily moisturiser with sun protection included.

Scent-sational

You don't just want to use Mother Nature's assets to feel good and look good, you want to smell good too – as good as an English country garden on a spring day, a freshly mown lawn or an ocean breeze perhaps. And we can't always rely on our naturally occurring pheromones to help us along. Well hooray, then, for the marriage of nature and science, because now the delectable fragrances of the great outdoors have been harnessed into bottles and oils to leave our nostrils – and the nostrils of our neighbours – singing all day. Many natural perfumes, which are free from the drying, strong alcohol content of some chemical concoctions, can be found online and in stores.

Choose one of these sweet scent styles found in nature to complete your divine being.

- **Aromatic** For a sweet and spicy scent, try a perfume with notes of rosemary, thyme, mint, tarragon, cinnamon, clove, ginger or cardamom.
- **Citrus** For a fresh and tangy scent, try a perfume with

notes of lemon, lime, orange, grapefruit, tangerine, bergamot or mandarin.

- **Floral** For a romantic and sweet scent, try a perfume with notes of lily-of-the-valley, rose, jasmine, tuberose, violet, carnation, gardenia or orange blossom.
- **Green** For a mild and fresh scent, try a perfume with notes of fresh leaves and grass.
- **Oceanic** For a light and airy scent, try a perfume with notes of (synthetic, sadly) mountain air, clean linen, sea breeze or ocean mist.
- **Woody** For an earthy and mossy scent, try a perfume with notes of cedar, sandalwood, patchouli or oak moss.

Mother Nature's make-up

- Stain lips with raspberries
- Pinch your cheeks – it works
- Gloss lips with pomegranate oil
- Even your skin tone (goodbye foundation) with ylang ylang flower oil
- Remove redness (goodbye concealer) with aloe vera gel
- Dry up spots with tea tree oil

A forest of fitness

The regular practice of forest therapy – or beach therapy or mountain therapy – gives you the anti-ageing benefits of fresh air and the ability to de-stress and chill out. It also helps you to stay trim and healthy. There is a reason why forest therapists refer to the woods as the 'green gym' and a lake or river as the 'blue gym'. The benefits of exercise, even gentle exercise as advocated in *Forest Therapy*, such as walking, swimming, yoga and stretching, are amplified when they're taken outside. Light exercise in the great outdoors helps to control body fat, tone muscles and strengthen bones in the same way that it would if you were working out on a staid, dull treadmill or in a grey weights room. Getting outdoors in the sunshine whenever possible, research shows, triggers increased belly fat-burning.

The dose of fresh air will also help you to sleep better, and getting a regular seven to eight hours per night of good-quality, deep shut-eye helps to regulate blood sugar levels and keep hunger and appetite hormones in balance. We all know how we reach for the doughnuts and sugary coffees after a late night. With a healthy forest-therapeutic approach to fresh air, healthy living and sleep, you won't need to.

Exercising outdoors improves healthy circulation, which gives skin that warm glow and naturally rosy-cheeked look we desperately desire as we get older.

Regular exercise has a positive effect on the telomeres. What are they? They are bundles of DNA that cap the chromosomes, and the longer they are, the less likely you are to have conditions such as obesity, diabetes, dementia and cardiovascular disease.

Research has shown that active people have chromosomes the same length as those ten years younger who are more sedentary. Turning back the clock by taking a turn around the park is a pretty easy way to relive your youth internally and externally, no?

Mother Nature has given us a glorious playground to explore and be active in, which will reduce sluggishness and lethargy, and make working out an adventure rather than a chore. Seriously, as I've said before, I am not a fitness freak. My natural position is seated, with a book, under a tree. But when I am out walking along a sandy stretch of beautiful beach, or climbing a lush hill to reach a wonderful panoramic view, I don't even notice the effort or the energy I'm expelling. I'm too busy soaking in the pleasing, invigorating aspects of my *friluftsliv* life.

MINDFULNESS MINUTE

During a soak in the bath, filled to the brim with some of the beautifying treats mentioned in this chapter, work your face into a series of stretches. Release tension and pressure by going through a series of facial exercises – movements that feel good. Open your jaw wide, stretch, close and repeat ten times. Next lift your brows, furrow your brows, and repeat ten times. Then tilt your head back to look at the ceiling and make an exaggerated pucker as if you're kissing the sky, and repeat ten times. You won't look pretty doing this, but it feels good and moves ageing tension out of the face.

11

Food Glorious Food

'One cannot think well, love well, sleep well,
if one has not dined well.'

Virginia Woolf

My brother and sister-in-law's home backs on to a woodland orchard in the Garden of England: Kent. Every spring and summer the landscape, surrounded by farms and interrupted occasionally by church steeples and oast houses, bursts into life with fruits, berries and vegetables. My niece and nephews jump into the ripening feast every afternoon straight from school, running wild from their house to pluck snacks from thorny hedgerows bursting with rubies. They return sated, their fingertips and tongues stained red from their forest fare, arms full of apples, pears, cherries and plums for pie-making and jam-preserving. In autumn and winter, they gather baskets of broad beans, kale and onions to stock hearty stews and soups.

It is an idyllic way to grow up, to be so aware of the countryside stirring through its cycles of renewal and retreat, and the different bounties each season offers, but this awareness is something we can all aspire to – orchard or not. To bring the colours, fragrances, health benefits and beauty of the wild to our plate, to decorate our tables with burgeoning buds and pretty petals, is to welcome Mother Nature to take a seat with us as we indulge in one of life's greatest pleasures: food.

Al fresco awesomeness

Mother Nature's favourite meal has to be the picnic, a time she really gets to join in the dining experience. But, too often, for humans, the idea of a picnic is better than the reality. Soggy sandwiches and pestering wasps, stinging nettles and snatching seagulls, mud patches and cowpats, sudden downpours or scorching sun. Eating outdoors isn't all sweet meadows and posh hampers. But you can improve your chances of making your life a picnic, relishing the great outdoors rather than cursing it, by planning ahead.

1   **Choose a location that lifts the soul**, off the beaten path: a quiet corner of a city park, a tourist-free beach cove, a mountain offering a glorious view. But be practical, especially if you have children. Are there

toilets nearby? Will you be forced to drag your feast miles from a parking spot, over nooks and stiles, trying not to spill your eatables? Do you have older people with you who won't be comfortable on a blanket on the ground? Should you bring portable chairs?

2 **Weatherproof your fare** Invest in a blanket with a waterproof back. Keep food dry and fresh with proper flasks, containers and wrapping. Bring wellies and umbrellas – a huge golf one can offer multiple people protection at one time – if the weather looks like it's turning. Also, prepare for the alternative with sunscreen, hats, sunglasses and plenty of water. And insect spray! Always remember insect spray, whatever the weather!

3 **Prepping and planning the food** is the fun bit, but don't forget the provisions you need to make it a proper meal: a small chopping board, cutlery, napkins, insulated glasses, condiments (salt, pepper and ketchup) and a bag to throw rubbish into. If you're planning a sunset picnic, remember candles and blankets. Many a summer's picnic in the countryside has been spoilt by a bottle of unopened wine, so don't forget the corkscrew.

4 **Cheating is fine** Go to a local farmers' market or delicatessen and buy it all in one go, to go. Especially during the summer months, bakers and farm shops cater deliciously to the picnic market and know how to avoid anything that goes soggy or stale after a few hours outdoors.

5   **Once you've eaten**, the day will be improved by some
    fun activities. Pack a kite, a Frisbee, bocce balls, a
    rounders bat and ball, a boomerang, some fishing
    nets if you're going near water (and waterproof shoes),
    a portable speaker for some chill-out tunes, a pack of
    cards. If you have children with you, lead them away
    on an adventure. My children and their friends are
    into bear hunts, witch hunts, ghost hunts and secret
    spy missions at the moment.

6   **Eat, drink, play, relax**, then leave the location exactly
    as you found it, taking litter with you if there are no
    available bins.

Blooming delicious

Eating flowers – which is believed to have begun in China more
than 3,000 years ago – has been a decadent way to decorate your
dinner, share a treat, or bring the healing powers of nature to
the table in Britain for centuries. In Medieval times, herbalists
put edible blooms into elixirs, potions and medicines, believ-
ing they could cure a raft of ills. In the Elizabethan age John
Gerard, the author of a definitive book on edible flowers, *Herball*,
or *Generall Historie of Plantes*, wrote: 'A syrup made of the floures
of borage comforteth the heart, purgeth melancholy and qui-
eteth the lunaticke person.' Later, during Queen Victoria's reign,
wooing gentlemen would bestow boxes of candied violets in the
hands of their sweethearts as a token of their eternal love, lust
and good intentions.

Modern scientific research has discovered that our

ancestors often knew what they were talking about, and that flowers and plants can benefit our diets, not just sass up the look of our sustenance with their beauty; for example, a study of the borage plant – aka the starflower mentioned by Gerard – found that there is a chemical produced in the flowers that, when consumed, stimulates the adrenal glands, which encourages the body to produce more adrenalin. This provides a pick-me-up when we feel tired and makes us feel better able to handle tough situations. Unsurprisingly then, in Roman times, the borage plant was known as the 'herb of courage', given to soldiers before battles, lacing their tea or wine with flowery power.

But it's not all coming up roses. You have to be very careful and knowledgeable before stuffing some petals into your casserole. Some flowers can make you very sick, as can the pesticides or other chemicals used on them. Source them responsibly, and never munch down on flowers grown on a roadside. Before sampling anything, identify not only the plant but also the part of the plant that is edible. And with edible flowers, you must remember that less is more, as over-eating can give you tummy troubles.

With all that said, they are having a resurgence in restaurants and resorts. I'm writing this chapter from an organic horse ranch, farm and orchard out in the Texas heartland. Here, wildflower pastures are cultivated – alongside 42 acres of herb gardens, berry patches and hormone-, fertiliser- and pesticide-free farmland – to wow the field-to-fork diners who stop by for a fresh, earthy taste of the Lone Star state. Sorrel, rosemary, cucumber and squash flowers compete to be the prettiest on my plate. You cannot help but smile when your lunch comes with a posy on it. Here are some other popular petals that are safe and look or taste good:

- **Cornflower** The delicate pale-blue flowers pretty up plates but taste quite bland. They are great for decorating more than for their flavour.
- **Dianthus** Usually spotted in quaint cottage gardens, these blooms are most often used as cake decorations, but they also last well in liquid, so add them to a drink for a splash of colour in a summer cocktail.
- **Fuchsia** A bit acidic on the tongue, but the bright, eye-catching colours and elegant shapes make them great for decoration. The blooms and berries are edible.
- **Garden sorrel** Use this tart treat instead of lemon for an exotic twist on citrus fruit – perfect for salads, sauces and squeezed over a rocket pizza.
- **Hibiscus** has a cranberry-like taste with a citrus bite. Dry the flowers to make a refreshing tea and use the petals lightly as a garnish for salads.
- **Honeysuckle** Whatever you do, don't eat the berries, which are highly poisonous, but the flowers, as you can imagine from the divine smell, taste of the sweetest honey.
- **Marigold**, aka calendula, have orange and yellow petals that are a little bitter. They are more often used by homeopaths in tinctures, creams, teas and salves for wounds, as the flower promotes rapid healing and prevents infection.
- **Nasturtium** Inside the horn-shaped flower, a sweet nectar awaits to be squeezed and sucked out. The

bright petals can be used to garnish salads.

- **Pansy** is an early spring treat for pretty floral displays and cake decorating.
- **Perennial phlox** It is the *perennial* phlox, not the *annual*, that is edible. Don't get them confused, your tummy will pay for it. It has a spicy taste, which is great to add flavour and colour – white, red, purple, pink – to your chow.
- **Primrose**, aka cowslip, these blooms are slightly sweet and add a colour boost to salads and cold dishes. They can also be pickled or fermented as wine.
- **Rose** The classic cake decoration, especially for weddings and christenings. The perfume can be harnessed for cake filling, ice cream and icing. Add the petals to a sugar syrup, bring to the boil and steep overnight, then drain.
- **Snapdragon** An acquired taste, snapdragon adds a bitter flavour but a handsome look.
- **Tulip** A decorative delight, the flower's big, strong petals can be used as containers to hold sauces, jams, dips and mousses.
- **Viola** These mini pansies are just as colourful and tasty as their big sister, and they are ready to eat in autumn and early winter.

Think before you drink

Pretty up your Pimm's by adding the outside to the inside of your glass. Freeze edible flowers, fruits and berries – even some herbs such as basil leaves – and chuck a couple of cubes into your sundowner for a drink that looks fresh and wild enough to roam in. Want to go a step further? Simply freeze individual petals and leaves (non-poisonous ones, of course – make sure to double check) in a freezer bag, then sprinkle them directly onto your divine libation. Herbal tea ice cubes with paired-up leaves or petals also make an elegant, tasty cool-down sip.

Entertaining each season

Food isn't just about stuffing your face and filling a hole – it is central to the art of celebration, happiness and connection, and it can be made all the more memorable and delicious when paired with the great outdoors. So, beyond what you serve, think about how you serve it. Make a meal an occasion by using each season as your guide to style – anything from a romantic picnic to a family reunion – with individuality, fun and comfort at its core.

Spring flings

- If printing invitations to an event, do so on handmade paper decorated with pressed spring flowers.
- Make the most of a gentle spring breeze by dangling Tibetan bells, dreamcatchers and beads around your garden, or under the tree where you're having your picnic.
- Tie brightly coloured ribbons around tree trunks where you'll be gathering.
- Get your Moana on and wear fresh flowers in your hair. You can be the host with the most and the host with the horticultural touch.
- A sprig of fresh blossom placed on each napkin is a nice touch.
- Instead of floral table arrangements, try bowls of hardy fruits such as lemons, pomegranates, limes and oranges.
- Gingham in pastel shades nudges memories of farm visits as a child, lambing season and chirping chicks. Use this pattern for a tablecloth and napkins, inside and out. Go all out at Easter. It's the only other time, apart from Christmas, that more is more and colours and sparkle should steal the show from the food itself. Dye eggs in different shades and place them as a centrepiece on tables. Make edible bird's nests out of breakfast cereal, bonded with melted chocolate and fill with sugar-coated chocolate eggs to leave on each placemat.
- Fill Kilner jars with pebbles, water, mini lily pads and blossom as centrepieces.
- Allow guests to make their own cordials. Leave out

a variety of flavours in different colours in crystal decanters, with an ice bucket, and still and sparkling water.

- Forget heavy dinners, serve an afternoon tea – delicate cakes and finger sandwiches decorated with mustard and cress and springtime edible flowers – it's easily transported in a hamper from home to garden if the weather allows. Or go for the more rustic farmhouse tea, serving platters of meats, cheeses and chutneys, scones and clotted cream, on family-style trestle tables.

Summer shindigs

- Throw a Hawaiian-themed party, day or night. Flip-flops, bright flowery shirts and leis required. Decorate the table with seashells and serve coconut cocktails in Tiki cups. If you have one, a surfboard lying horizontal would make a fun bar. Shaved ice is the treat of the islands, so invest in a slushy machine for a cooling treat.
- For a garden party, thread seashells with string and hang them in the summer breeze. Use glitter spray for sunset sparkle.
- On a very hot day, for a special occasion where you want everyone outside, think about providing parasols, fans or shady spots for guests. Wigwams and teepees are having a moment and are getting prettier and cheaper by the day, too.
- Ornate bowls of blue water filled with floating candles and petals makes a Zen-like water garden.

- A Raj-style tent in bedazzling jewel colours will make an extra room in the garden if you're short on space. Give the area a specific purpose: chill-out zone, bar area or dance floor.
- Two words: fairy lights. During long, hot summer evenings spent outdoors, you can never have too many fairy lights.
- Move your barbecue away from burgers, sausages and curdled coleslaw and into the sweet Southern style of pulled pork, brisket and green beans. Bourbon is the drink to offer alongside this – a warming, sweet cocktail like a Manhattan is perfect for a summer's night.
- Leave sticks of candy-striped rock on place settings, napkins or in jars next to the bar for some retro sweetness.
- Bunting on a summer's day is the most charming thing, reminiscent of summer fêtes of yesteryear. String it between trees for a country-charm look.
- Paint pebbles you've found on the beach as place markers for people, or fold paper boats to write people's names on.
- Make pitchers of iced-cold lemonade and serve with cheese and crackers. The combo works, I promise.
- Thinking about hiring entertainment? Nothing says summer fun quicker than a steel drum band, and the rhythmic melodies take you to the beach in a second. It's a real treat if you're throwing your gathering in a city. Salsa or samba tunes will do the same.
- Serve mini portions of fish and chips in old newspaper (minus the seagulls).
- Go back to your youth. Provide a selection of water

pistols, water balloons and a paddling pool for guests to have fun with.

- Evenings do get chilly, even in August, so if you want guests to hover outside in the great outdoors, do think about providing blankets or outdoor heaters, or see if you could make a bonfire.
- Have a popsicle party. Make your own ice lollies from fresh fruit juice and herbal tea, stuffed with natural beautifiers such as berries, or buy some. Everyone loves a lick.

Autumn amusements

- As the nights draw in, light up your soirées with candles. Be inventive. Tea lights in pumpkins, grand candelabras, clusters of church candles in corners. Be safe and be scented – burn autumnal scents like cinnamon and pumpkin.
- Use the variety of fallen coloured leaves and twigs – and orange and silver glitter spray – to decorate mantelpieces and tables.

- Shine up some conkers and tie them with a mini name-tag for place settings.
- Carve pumpkins and place in groups at the entrance to your gathering, in the loo, or as a table centrepiece.
- Partying on Guy Fawkes Night? Put mini sparklers into cocktails and desserts, then hand out normal-sized sparklers after dinner with dark chocolate mints and coffee to take out into the garden.
- A candyfloss or popcorn machine offers all the fun of the fair at your house.
- Apple-bobbing for adults isn't elegant, but it is fun. Set up a booth in the garden.
- Make a DIY jacket potato stand: pile up the spuds and leave out with dishes of help-yourself baked beans, cheese, butter, chilli con carne and soured cream.
- Serve mini toad-in-the-holes as bite-sized treats if you're throwing a cocktail party.
- At a Halloween dinner party, leave tricks (like consequences or have-you-ever question cards) and treats (like little bags of orange and brown M&Ms or caramel corn) at each guest's place setting. This will entertain between courses.
- Serve monster cocktails for a spooky night – green slime optional, but if you can get smoke climbing out of the glass like the zombies from 'Thriller', you win.
- As a leaving gift, give guests mini pots of autumnal fruit jams or compotes. Gooseberry and blackberry always go down well.

Winter winners

- Make your home feel snug and reassuring for your guests by using candlelit lanterns dotted along the front path to your house or flat.
- Serve cups of steaming cider or mulled wine, garnished with cinnamon sticks and orange slices.
- Pin red sequins or buttons and green fern leaves to napkins.
- This is the season for sparkle and magic. Don't be shy: fairy lights, glitter, candles, sequins – don't hold back. Dress for the part of host in as much glitz as you can handle.
- Berries and twigs, lightly doused in fake snow, make a festive centrepiece. Drape ivy or mistletoe from the backs of chairs. In fact, for a merry Christmas gathering, tie mistletoe everywhere.
- If Jack Frost hasn't painted your windows yet, help him out by decorating them with a snowflake design.
- In December, hide dull areas of your home by hanging up stockings, tinsel and baubles. A real fir tree in the entrance will have wow factor, and the scent will welcome guests warmly.
- Leave fir cones or candy canes, with handwritten brown paper tags attached, as place markers at your dining table.
- At a party in the run-up to Christmas, crackers are a must. One per guest at least.
- An Arabian Nights theme – rich, decadent and

sumptuous – will warm up cold evenings. Fill a room with oversized cushions and wisely placed orange-scented candles.

- Serve port or sherry, and attempt eggnog. Decorate glasses with a rim of green, red, silver or gold edible sugar and a cluster of cranberries.
- Mini Yorkshire puddings filled with turkey and cranberry sauce, followed by bite-sized sticky toffee puddings, warm guests' tummies on a cold winter's night.
- Leave token gifts or a mini fir tree or cactus with a 'thank you for coming' tag in a Santa sleigh at the exit.
- Learn the words to 'Auld Lang Syne' if you're having a New Year's Eve party. There always needs to be a leader.
- Go against the norm and celebrate Galentine's Day, not Valentine's Day, in February. Gather all your favourite women – and their partners if you choose – in your garden for an evening of bonfires, hot chocolate and funny anecdotes about love.

Kiley, 36

'Hosting a sit-down dinner is complicated in general, but outside, in late spring, with weather forecasts for thunderstorms, I was leaving a lot up to fate. It had rained for 28 days straight. Yet I knew that getting married with my bare feet stretched out in the grass and passing food from one person to another had as much spiritual meaning to me as the words "I do", so it was an idea I wasn't going to give up on. Growing up, my goal was to be outside at all times, and that guided my principles and passions. Getting married was never a top priority, but caring for the earth and breaking bread with friends and family always was. You get the picture – Mother Nature had to have a seat at my table because she had such a profound hand in shaping me into the woman I am today. Luckily, the clouds parted and the sun shone on that evening in May. At 6pm friends and family gathered in our back garden among pine and oak trees. Even the paper we printed our programmes on could be planted. We ate farm fare of pulled pork and chicken. We passed cornbread and shared stories about my youth and that of my now husband. We laughed, we cried, we ate beneath the stars. The evening was perfect.'

Animal crackers

As a rather tired new mum living in a new city in the US, life could be a bit lonely and stressful and – as weirdly Cinderella as it sounds – after discovering our house was in a place abundantly inhabited by all kinds of birds and squirrels, I was cheered up by the chirping creatures I could see going about their business in my back garden. I set up a bird feeder and a water fountain outside my kitchen window so that as I did the washing up and mashed countless avocados, I could see rather cuter, fluffier mummies preparing dinners for their young. My children would coo at the wild guests too, especially on bad snow and ice days when it was too dangerous to take them out and our only visitors would be bright red cardinals and fluffy squirrels, perched, eyeball to eyeball with us.

Feed the birds

We need to be careful about what we feed, or don't feed, our furry friends, and the needs shift between breeds, species and seasons. For birds, autumn and winter is when human help is really needed, so do put food and water out on a regular basis – twice daily if the weather is severe. During these frosty days, give birds good-quality food – investigate specially formulated wild bird seed at a local pet or garden store, and ask what type of feeder would suit the birds in your area, your back garden and your commitment level. Clean the feeders of uneaten food every couple of days, and once you have set up a routine, try to stick to it.

In spring and summer, stick to a once-a-day routine and still be mindful of keeping the feeders clean. Avoid bread, peanuts and fat, or any other dry, hard foods that can be harmful to baby birds. Choking is a real hazard for them too, not just human babies. Despite what we've grown up thinking, bread is never a good idea, as it offers no nutrition, and mouldy bread is harmful. Pay attention to how much food is left at the end of the day and adjust the quantity you leave out accordingly.

Place feeders away from bushes or trees where predatory cats could be lurking, and perhaps don't encourage birds to hang out in your garden if you share your home with cats and dogs. Place feeders within three feet of a window so that they won't be speeding towards glass but slowing down to rest on the feeder – and you will be able to enjoy looking at them as they feast. All year round, if you're hoping to attract wildlife to your garden, avoid toxic sprays, and pay attention when mowing the lawn to avoid small creatures that might be in the grass.

Rules for feeding time at your garden zoo

- Use good-quality food.
- Don't encourage animals to eat from your hand, and don't encourage them into your home.
- Keep feeding utensils, feeders and tables clean and hygienic.
- Don't attract badgers or foxes into your garden with food if hedgehogs are breeding in your or a neighbour's garden. Do note that badgers eat hedgehogs and that its unusual to have hedgehogs and badgers in the same area.
- Feed each animal the appropriate amount of food. Over-feeding can cause changes in their natural behaviour and socialisation. They may also become over-reliant on you so that if you go away they are unable to find an alternative in such a large quantity.

If you've having Mrs Tiggywinkle and her chums to tea . . .

Hedgehogs like peanuts, mixed seeds and dried fruit used as ground-feed for birds. These can be scattered on your lawn. Tinned dog and cat foods are fine, but fish-based food goes off very quickly. Bread and milk gives hedgehogs diarrhoea so avoid at all costs. Grey squirrels can bully other wildlife, so if you feel inclined, keep them at bay from bird feeders using baffles (these are cones attached to bird feeders at a height to which squirrels cannot jump). If you are lucky enough to have the smaller, rarer red squirrels, they can be fed using a hopper with a treadle that stops the heavier grey squirrels from gaining access, or you can use a feeder with an entrance that is too small for them to squeeze through.

Badgers like peanuts, dog food, bread and cheese. Mice and voles enjoy mixed grain. In severe winters, deer may enter your garden looking for food if you live in the country, but if you encourage them, you do risk your garden being trampled on. If feeding them is more important than your lawn, they enjoy cereals, carrots and hay. Foxes will eat almost anything, from meat scraps to cake, but they particularly love peanuts. If you find that food is attracting rats make sure you only put food at a high level (for birds) and don't leave anything out at night, which is when rats tend to go to find food (more info on RSPB website).

MINDFULNESS MINUTE

Eating nourishes the soul, and lovingly preparing a meal for yourself, or friends and family, should be therapeutic too. Make yourself a rainbow plate to brighten a dull day. On a large plate, place seven different-coloured fruits, salads or vegetables in circles. Let your eyes take in the prettiness, then let your stomach enjoy the colourful harvest. A beautiful platter of shades would be strawberries, tangerine segments, honeydew melon balls, figs, blueberries, plums and cherries. Bon appétit!

12

The Call of the Wild

'Adopt the pace of nature: her secret is patience.'

Ralph Waldo Emerson

As an exhausted fortysomething parent, who recently lost her last grandparent and is recovering from a health scare, the importance of the lessons from the last 11 chapters has been particularly relevant to me. All too often in my recent history, life and death, fear and pain have grabbed me by the throat and shaken the need for change into my soul – and then some. You might be realising that you need to make some changes too, to any or all aspects of your life, going forward. That you need to gain the good – the quality time in nature, self-care and solitude, meaningful relationships with people you care about – and lose the bad, like worrying over things you can't control or wasting time on people, places and things that aren't good for your mental or physical health.

A life well lived

The deathbed scenario can be a useful mental exercise, too. On your deathbed, what will you wish you spent *more* time doing, and what will you wish you spent *less* time doing? You won't regret seeing that sunset with your partner and the way your hands found each other as a warm glow descended over the horizon. You won't regret those Sunday walks with your children when they were small and mesmerised by the world unfolding in front of them. You won't regret those rather wild beach holidays you took with your friends as a teenager. You'll yearn to go back to these moments – even for a second – and feel what you felt back then. Your heart will be stretched between joy that you lived those times, and sadness that you can't repeat them.

On your deathbed, you will regret not looking after your health, you will regret being on your phone too much, and you will regret spending too many late nights in the office. You will regret telling the people you love what they mean to you. You will regret beating yourself up over things you couldn't change. You will regret not opening your heart to all that this world has to offer.

Please don't wait until it's too late. Start living the life you deserve today.

How to embrace a happier you right now

What kind of person do you want to be? You want to be a happy and healthy person, am I right? And the previous chapters of this book have hopefully given you some useful ideas on how you can be that with the help of forest therapy, quality time with good people, the changing seasons and Mother Nature. That's not to say hugging a tree or taking a walk along the coast will clear your mind of all worries and fears. Some things are too sad, too difficult or too painful to be blown away on the breeze, but things can be improved. Dark moments can be brightened and mental loads lightened when we begin to value ourselves and surround ourselves with things that we know are good for our mental and physical well-being: family who love us, friends who value us, landscapes that make our hearts soar, and rituals that give us a sense of contentment, peace and joy. These things help us through the moments that knock the wind out of our sails and push us to the ground. It takes time – it took me until my forties – but we can all learn to embrace change, appreciate the gifts we've been given, accept that the challenges we face are lessons to make us a braver, kinder or stronger person, and walk through the day-to-day routines that can feel laborious and repetitive with a calm understanding that some tasks just need to be completed for our world to go on turning.

Biophilia vs biophobia

Many of us need a wake-up call and an attitude adjustment. Too many of us have been living in fear or pain – or just at an unnecessarily uninspired level – without even realising it. We need to get off the fence – even if it is in the garden – and chose a side. And the side we choose should be to embrace nature and our best self. Here are two terms to help you decide how you want to see the world and how you want to see yourself.

ARE YOU A BIOPHILE?

- Do you feel an emotional, empathetic attachment to nature and other living things?
- Do you have a love of life and feel driven to preserve yourself and those around you?
- Whenever you meet a puddle do you yearn to jump into it, or when you see a flower do you feel the need to sniff it? Have you ever been left speechless by a mountain view or the sound of the ocean?

If you answered YES to all these, you are a biophile. Being a biophile means feeling a strong attraction for the living world and everything in it.   ▶

ARE YOU A BIOPHOBE?

- Do you feel an aversion to nature, a dislike for the outdoors?
- Do you have a distaste for mud, sudden rainstorms or feeling sand between your toes?
- Are you scared by what you can't control? Nervous of things you don't understand?

If you answered YES to all these, you are a biophobe. Being a biophobe means ignoring your ancestors and ignoring your grandchildren – and, most worryingly, ignoring the easy, quick, cost-free ways you have at your disposal to feel sunny and upbeat today. Read this book again and become a biophile.

Evie, 46

'During the few times in my life when I have been broken and profoundly sad, it has been nature that has healed me. Getting lost in the forest – a walking meditation – seems to melt my human troubles away. The overwhelming beauty. The remoteness. The possibility of danger. The timelessness. All these exceed any of my temporal obstacles. Nature can heal us, and help us to escape ourselves.'

Forests in your future

How can you serve and cherish your relationship with nature going forward? Clearly, there are imperative, urgent changes we need to make as individuals, communities, countries and as human beings, to protect our planet. We need to tweak our daily habits, re-educate ourselves and our children, and start to think in the long term about what we can do to help the environment. But, very simply, you can make small, impactful improvements to your life and the lives of those around you by becoming a champion for outdoor living. Try some of these:

- Help to run, or start, a gardening club at a local school or park in your neighbourhood, or at a senior care home or homeless centre.
- Join the board of volunteers at a local park, public gardens, allotment club, wildlife centre or historic home.
- With permission from the relevant authorities, plant trees or plants to beautify your local area.
- Start a vegetable patch or herb garden in your back garden. If you can't do that, choose to support your local farmers' market or farm shop wherever possible.
- Set up a local walking, jogging, nature-mindfulness or cycling group.
- Start to compost and recycle.
- Change how you use water, electricity, plastic and your car. Reduce, reduce, reduce.
- Contact your local council about their environmental programmes and get on board.

- Be mindful of how you run your home and garden, for the improvement of those around you and the planet. What can you add? What can you take away?
- Keep your local area tidy by picking up litter, and set up groups to do the same.
- Teach your parents, children and neighbours about World Earth Day – throw a party, do a film night. Or gather friends and family to celebrate each changing season, or the summer or winter solstice.
- Donate your time, money or ideas to organisations that encourage environmental protection and the celebration of nature in an area you are passionate about: the sea, farming, animal welfare. Follow your heart.
- Keep a collection of anecdotes, stories, photos and pictures about nature and the impact it's had on your family, and make it into a scrapbook to hand down to the next generation.

- Build traditions within your family or friendship group that champion outdoor pursuits, from weekly hikes at a local beauty spot to an annual camping trip in a forest glen that you all look forward to every year.

Gabrielle, 38

'Having a strong connection to the mountains is in my blood. My father, a New Yorker, moved out to the Rocky Mountains a few years before I was born. When I was growing up, he would take us skiing, hiking and snowshoeing. Until his death early last year, his daily routine included a short hike up the ridge near to my childhood home before putting on his work shoes and heading in to see patients as one of our town's first family doctors. As he was dying, we set his bed to face out on to the mountain range east of our house. He passed away looking at one of his favourite views. Per his request, some of his ashes were scattered at the top of one of his favourite hikes, others were scattered along that ridge he hiked to start each day, and the rest were split among his children, which we have each scattered on mountains or hills close to our own homes. Now, when I want to talk to him or just feel his presence, I lace up my hiking boots and head into nature. And after doing so independently and instinctually on the first birthday since his passing, my siblings and I now 'Summit for Pop' on his birthday, his death anniversary, and Father's Day.'

True colours

Colour therapy – aka chromotherapy – is a jubilant way to bring the outdoors into your interior, to embrace shades from nature that have brought you a sense of peace and well-being and to use them to decorate your home to make it even happier. Make mental notes of your favourite shades when you are out on a forest walk, or by the sea – perhaps take photos to hold the tone in your mind – then reinterpret them and their positive effects on you through paint, meaningful artwork and objects that make you cheerful or chilled. Use colours from nature to create the world you want to live in, even when you can't be outside.

- **Blue** Bring the sea and sky to your four walls. Light to mid-colour shades of blue are relaxing, spiritually uplifting and peaceful – perfect for areas of quiet contemplation.
- **Green** The quintessential colour of nature – trees, grass, moss and meadows – green works well in all domestic spaces. Use anywhere you want to promote feelings of health, harmony and well-being.
- **Lavender** Calming and restful, lavender is perfect for bedrooms or rooms in your home where you like to sit, read or meditate as if relaxing in a field of wild flowers.
- **Orange** Bright like the sun, use orange for a warm and lively feel. Add it to the most sociable room in your home for a rejuvenating place to hang out.
- **Red** As romantic as a scarlet rose, this colour can make

an area warm and cosy (sexy, even) but can be claustrophobic and heavy in the wrong space, so proceed with caution.

- **Yellow** Like an invigorating walk across golden sand, this colour makes us feel bright, confident and pumped up for mental or physical activity. It's great for social rooms such as dining areas and sitting rooms, but avoid it in bedrooms, as it might make you feel too alert to doze off.

How to maintain a relationship with Mother Nature in trying times

Sometimes we don't feel peppy and energetic, positive or brave. Sometimes we crumple, crumble and want to hide away, usually indoors, sometimes under a duvet, out of the sun. At these times, you have two options:

1   To remember how much better you'll feel getting outdoors into nature.
2   To bring the power of nature into your home.

To live the first option, you need to harness flashbacks and get a sense of self-awareness, to remember how much stronger and happier you felt when you did get outdoors and embrace nature. Your mood improved, your energy levels rose, your anxiety defused. And you need to recall how maintaining a nurturing relationship with Mother Nature curtails a myriad of downers, making you more creative, smarter, fitter, nicer with boosted immunity and heart health, and ultimately, studies show, more likely to live a long and happy life. Remembering all this could motivate you to get outdoors.

To live the second option, you need to welcome Mother Nature into your home as a guest while you're feeling physically or mentally unable to go and visit her. Use photos, paintings and drawings to surround yourself visually with her beauty. Coat your hideaway with her stress-relieving scents – in your bubble bath, in an essential-oil facial mist, in aromatherapy candles. Treat yourself to a bunch of flowers every weekend. Nurture pot plants or window boxes and hang air plants. Reminisce about favourite moments in the wild, and daydream the day away. Practise the mindfulness you engage in the natural world at home, making a spot that is just for you to be quiet and comforted in. Research shows that just looking at photos of nature or smelling the scents of nature has a positive effect on mental health.

Young at heart

Ultimately, I truly believe, we all have the wish and desire – and the power – to be our best, most blissful selves when we embrace the great outdoors. I know this because we were born this way. As children:

We were explorers
We were enquirers
We were risk-takers
We were caretakers
We were seeking happiness
We were seeking movement, freedom and good health

... and, as children, we knew that nothing felt as good as jumping in a puddle, jumping in waves or getting caught in the rain. And in those moments, we were – and we can still be, even as adults – our best, truest, happiest and bravest selves.

MINDFULNESS MINUTE

Take yourself to a favourite spot in nature, somewhere you can sit quietly and comfortably without fear of interruption or feeling restricted. Close your eyes, breathe in and out, and settle your body into the ground. Feel your way through each limb, bone and muscle. Ease out stiffness and focus on the sound and rhythm of your inhaling and exhaling. Capture yourself in your mind's eye – your best self. Give yourself a good look over, notice how you're standing, how you're smiling, how you're interacting with the world around you. Now, travel into your thoughts. Acknowledge how you feel, how you want to feel, what makes you happy. Capture this you for the future. Capture the essence of your happiness, individuality, kindness and energy. Open your eyes feeling lucky about who you are, where you are, and the control you have over your future.

Further

Further Reading

Books

Almon, Joan, *Playing It Up: With Loose Parts, Playpods, and Adventure Playgrounds*, CreateSpace, 2017

Clifford, M. Amos, *The Little Handbook of Shinrin-yoko*, www.Shinrin-Yoku.org, 2013

Gardner, Howard and Katie Davis, *The App Generation: How Today's Youth Navigate Identity, Intimacy, and Imagination in a Digital World*, Yale University Press, 2014

Jordan, Martin and Joe Hinds, *Ecotherapy: Theory, Research and Practice*, Palgrave, 2016

Louv, Richard, *Last Child in the Woods: Saving our Children from Nature-Deficit Disorder*, Atlantic Books, 2010

McGeeney, Andy, *With Nature in Mind: The Ecotherapy Manual for Mental Health Professionals*, Jessica Kingsley Publishing, 2016

Palmer, Sue, *Toxic Childhood: How the Modern World is Damaging Our Children and What We Can Do About It*, Orion, 2006.

Weaver, Dr Libby, *Rushing Woman's Syndrome*, Hay House, 2017

Williams, Florence, *The Nature Fix: Why Nature Makes Us Happier, Healthier, and More Creative*, W. W. Norton & Company, 2017

Helpful websites

To find out more about the National Trust, go to
nationaltrust.org.uk

To find out more about English Heritage, go to
english-heritage.org.uk

To find out more about the Wildlife Trust, go to
wildlifetrusts.org

To find out more about horticultural therapy, go to
Thrive.org.uk

For latest news, advice and research into health and recreation in
England, go to Public Health England at gov.uk/government/
organisations/public-health-england

For more information about feeding birds and wildlife, go to
rspb.org.uk or discoverwildlife.com

For more science and statistics

Akers, A., Barton, J., Cossey, R., et al. (2012), 'Visual color
perception in green exercise: Positive effects on mood
and perceived exertion', *Environmental Science and
Technology*, 46(16): 8661–6, http://www.ncbi.nlm.nih.gov/
pubmed/22857379

Aspinall, P., Mavros, P., Coyne, R., Roe, J. (2012), 'The urban brain:
analyzing outdoor physical activity with mobile EEG', *British
Journal of Sports Medicine*, http://www.ncbi.nlm.nih.gov/
pubmed/23467965

Barton, J., Pretty, J. (2010), 'What is the best dose of nature and
green exercise for improving mental health? A multi-study
analysis', *Environmental Science and Technology*, 44: 3947–55,
http://www.ncbi.nlm.nih.gov/pubmed/20337470

Berman, M.G., Jonides, J., Kaplan, S., (2008), 'The cognitive benefits of interacting with nature', *Psychological Science*, 19: 1207–12. http://libra.msra.cn/Publication/6994981/ the-cognitive-benefits-of-interacting-with-nature

Children and Nature Network (2012), 'Health Benefits to Children from Contact with the Outdoor & Nature', 46 pages, http://www.childrenandnature.org/downloads/ CNNHealthBenefits2012.pdf.

Donovan, G. Butry, D. Michael, Y., et al.. (2013), 'The relationship between trees and human health: Evidence from the spread of the EAB', *American Journal of Preventive Medicine*, 44(2): 139–45, http://californiareleaf.org/trees-in-the-news/ the-relationship-between-trees-human-health

Gies, E. (2006), 'The Health Benefits of Parks', The Trust for Public Land, http://www.tpl.org/publications/books-reports/park-benefits/the-health-benefits-of-parks.html

Hanson, P., Matt, F., Bowyer, J., et al. (2016), 'The Human Health and Social Benefits of Urban Forests', Dovetail Partners Inc. (1 MB PDF, 12 pages)

Kuo, F.E., Taylor, A.F. (2004), 'A potential natural treatment for attention-deficit/hyperactivity disorder: Evidence from a national study', *American Journal of Public Health*, 94(9): 1580–86, http://www.ncbi.nlm.nih.gov/pmc/articles/pmc1448497/

Lee, J., Park, B.-J., Tsunetsugu, Y., et al. (2009), 'Restorative effects of viewing real forest landscapes, based on a comparison with urban landscapes', *Scandinavian Journal of Forest Research*, 24(3): 227–34, http://www.tandfonline.com/doi/abs/10.1080/028275 80902903341#preview

Lee, J., Park, B.-J., Tsunetsugu, Y., et al. (2011), 'Effect of forest bathing on physiological and psychological responses in young Japanese male subjects', *Public Health*, 125(2):

93–100, http://www.sciencedirect.com/science/article/pii/
S0033350610003203

Li, Q. (2010), 'Effect of forest bathing trips on human immune
function', *Environmental Health and Preventative Medicine*,
15(1): 9–17, http://www.ncbi.nlm.nih.gov/pmc/articles/
PMC2793341/

Li, Q., Kawada, T. (undated but probably 2010), 'Healthy forest
parks make healthy people: Forest environments enhance
human immune function', Department of Hygiene and
Public Health, Nippon Medical School, Tokyo, Japan, http://
www.hphpcentral.com/wp-content/uploads/2010/09/5000-
paper-by-Qing-Li2-2.pdf

Li, Q., Kobayashi, M., Kawada, T. (2008), 'Relationships between
percentage of forest coverage and standardized mortality
ratios (SMR) of cancers in all prefectures in Japan', *Open Public
Health Journal*, 1:1–7, http://www.benthamscience.com/open/
tophj/articles/V001/1TOPHJ.pdf

Li, Q., Kobayashi, M., Wakayama, Y., et al. (2009), 'Effect of
phytoncide from trees on human natural killer cell
function', *International Journal of Immunopathology and
Pharmacology*, 22(4): 951–9, http://europepmc.org/abstract/
MED/20074458/reload=0;jsessionid=BnlPLmTxArJ6VpF0s
4MU.6

Li, Q., Morimoto, K., Nakadai, A., et al. (2007), 'Forest bathing
enhances human natural killer activity and expression of
anti-cancer proteins', *International Journal of Immunopathology
and Pharmacology*, 20(2 Suppl. 2): 3–8, http://www.ncbi.nlm.
nih.gov/pubmed/17903349.

Li, Q., Nakadai, A., Matsushima, H., et al. (2006), 'Phytoncides
(wood essential oils) induce human natural killer cell

activity', *Immunopharmacology and Immunotoxicology*, 28: 319–33, http://www.ncbi.nlm.nih.gov/pubmed/16873099

Maas, J., Verheij, R., Groenewegen, P., et al. (2006), 'Greenspace, urbanity, and health: How strong is the relation?', *Journal of Epidemiology and Community Health*, 60(7): 587–92, http://www. ncbi.nlm.nih.gov/pmc/articles/PMC2566234/

Maller, C., Henderson-Wilson, C., Pryor, A., et al. (2008), 'Healthy parks, healthy people: The health benefits of contact with nature in a park context. A review of relevant literature', 2nd edn, Parks Victoria, http://parkweb.vic.gov.au/about-us/ healthy-parks-healthy-people/the-research. (Scroll to the bottom of the page for the document.)

Ohtsuka, Y., Yabunaka, N., Takayama, S. (1998), 'Shinrin-yoku (forest-air bathing and walking) effectively decreases blood glucose levels in diabetic patients', *International Journal of Biometeorology*, 41(3): 125–7, http://www.ncbi.nlm.nih.gov/ pubmed/9531856

Park, B.-J., Furuya, K., Kasetani, T., et al. (2011), 'Relationship between psychological responses and physical environments in forest settings', *Landscape and Urban Planning*, 102(1): 24–32, http://www.sciencedirect.com/science/article/pii/ S0169204611001368

Park, B.-J., Tsunetsugu, Y., Kasetani, T., et al. (2010), 'The physiological effects of Shinrin-yoku (taking in the forest atmosphere or forest bathing): Evidence from field experiments in 24 forests across Japan', *Environmental Health and Preventative Medicine*, 15(1): 18–26, http://www.ncbi.nlm. nih.gov/pubmed/19568835

Taylor, A.F., Kuo, F.E. (2009), 'Children with attention deficits concentrate better after a walk in the park', *Journal of*

Attention Disorders, 12(5): 402–49, http://jad.sagepub.com/content/12/5/402

Thompson, C.W., Roe, J., Aspinall, P., et al. (2012), 'More green space is linked to less stress in deprived communities: Evidence from salivary cortisol patterns', *Landscape and Urban Planning*, 105(3): 221–9, http://www.sciencedirect.com/science/article/pii/S0169204611003665

Townsend, M. (2008), 'Healthy parks, healthy people: The health benefits of contact with nature in a park context: A review of relevant literature', Deakin University, Burwood, Melbourne, Australia, http://parkweb.vic.gov.au/__data/assets/pdf_file/0018/313821/HPHP-deakin-literature-review.pdf

Tsunetsugu, Y., Lee, L., Park, B.-J., et al. (2013), 'Physiological and psychological effects of viewing urban forest landscapes assessed by multiple measurements', *Landscape and Urban Planning*, 113: 90–93, http://www.sciencedirect.com/science/article/pii/S0169204613000212

Tsunetsugu, Y., Park, B., Miyazaki, Y. (2010), 'Trends in research related to "Shinrin-yoku" (taking in the forest atmosphere or forest bathing) in Japan', *Environmental Health and Preventative Medicine*, 15(1): 27–37, http://www.ncbi.nlm.nih.gov/pmc/articles/PMC2793347/

Ulrich, R.S. (1999), 'Effects of gardens on health outcomes: Theory and research', in C. Cooper-Marcus and M. Barnes (eds), *Healing Gardens: Therapeutic Benefits and Design Recommendations*, New York: John Wiley, pp. 27–86, http://www.majorfoundation.org/pdfs/Effects%20of%20Gardens%20on%20Health%20Outcomes.pdf

Acknowledgements

To the wonderful group of people who made this book take flight, thank you – what a breath of fresh air you are! Zoe Ross, my agent, I love your enthusiasm, efficiency and effortless cool and I feel lucky to have you – and the rest of the stellar team at United Agents, especially global go-getters Alex Stephens and Georgina Le Grice – by my side.

To Jillian Young, who commissioned this book, and Anna Steadman, who lead it towards publication, you, your editorial excellence and your vision rock. Thanks to Jillian Stewart for weeding out the worries in the copy, and to Stephanie Melrose for your exciting ideas. Everyone at Piatkus and Little, Brown – you have been such a joy. I want to hang out on your rooftop terrace more please!

Ruth Craddock, my illustrator – I've loved your whimsical, charming illustrations for many years now and I'm so happy to have them decorating my words.

To the friends who shared their heart-warming or heart-breaking stories with me to include throughout my copy, your noted connections with nature are now my favourite part of the book and I'm so grateful for your honesty. Thanks to Rosie, who got me thinking that there was a book in this topic. And thanks to my fellow Highland Park Elementary and Crenshaw

Athletic Club parents who join me and my rascals in every kind of weather, every day, to let our wild things be wild in the open air.

To my fantastic family, gorgeous godchildren and firmest friends: you are my spring, summer, autumn and winter. Thank you for the year-round happiness you bring me!